Remembering Angie

"YOU NEVER GET THOSE DAYS BACK"

Alicia Hannah

Palmetto Publishing Group
Charleston, SC

Remembering Angie
Copyright © 2019 by Alicia Hannah

First Edition

Printed in the United States

Hardcover: 978-1-64111-484-4
Paperback: 978-1-64111-485-1
eBook: 978-1-64111-486-8

Angie Lynn Poma

Weighing in at 9cm x 5.2cm x 2.9cm

Noticed: Spring, 2016
Discovered: May 4, 2018
Evicted: August 15, 2018

ACKNOWLEDGMENTS

I would like to thank my mother and father, my children, Brooke and Johnathon; along with my extended family, my great friends, especially Kathy, Jay, Tommi, Beth, Josie, my Independence Middle School family, my brilliant doctors and their medical staff, along with Netflix for helping me survive this roller coaster. I feel humbled by all of the love and support and could not have survived this journey without you all! Lastly, a special thanks to Angie and her friends for the ride of my life! I will never forget you!

Angie, when I first noticed you it was early 2016. I asked my doctor, Dr. Rutkowski, about you as if you were something worth looking into. You were the size of a small walnut, yet not painful at all. My doctor said, "Let's keep an eye on it and see if it changes." The months passed, yet you were still a bothersome site to me. Since I hadn't gotten an answer from my doctor, I decided to go see my dermatologist, Dr. Cevasco, in November of the same year. I figured if my regular doctor didn't know, maybe someone who specializes in skin diseases would. To my surprise, he looked closely at you, touched you, looked at me and said, "This is not my area of expertise," and recommended I go back to my regular doctor, so I let you go for a while.

In February, 2017, I went for my yearly check up and again my doctor said, "Let's keep an eye on it, that it hadn't really changed, and that most likely it is what is called a lipoma."

"Thank goodness," I thought, "finally a name for you, a fatty little benign tumor." Once again, I thought life will go on, and you were nothing to worry about.

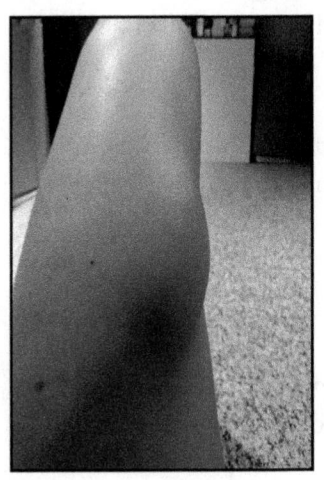

As the months passed and life went on, I began to notice you getting slightly bigger. It was in the fall of 2017 that my mother mentioned you might be growing as well. I put her comment in the back of my mind and went on with life. I continued my daily activities and workouts as usual. One evening, in early February 2018, I was doing sit-ups on my basement floor. I looked at my thigh, took a picture of you, and sent it to my mother. I think she panicked a bit and texted me to get you looked at ASAP. One afternoon as I continued my workouts at school with my colleagues/friends, Geri and Tommi, they also began to notice how you had grown and encouraged me, pretty adamantly I might add, to get you checked out. I believe we were all in shock that you started to look like I actually had a baby's head in my thigh. They were beginning to get very concerned and all but drove me to the ER. I promised I would go that night, and I did. After stopping home and letting the kids know I was heading to urgent care, I went in and asked if I could speak to someone about you and possibly get an MRI or a CT scan that day. When I met with the lady and I showed her my leg, she kind of sat back in disbelief. Again, I was told this was not her area of expertise, and I should go back to my regular doctor. Lol.

I made another appointment with Dr. Rutkowski.

FEB. 21

I went in for my check up at Dr. Rutkowski's office. Not only did I go for my yearly blood work, but to show him how you have grown. Once he checked me out and wrote out all of my yearly scripts, I said, "I also wanted to show you this again." I pointed to my thigh and he said, "Ohhhh my, we definitely need to have that looked at." He referred me to a general surgeon, Dr. Gemma, and he wrote a script for an MRI. I ran down to the MRI room in the same building in my shorts and socks, carrying my shoes, to get it done right then and there. But unfortunately, I could not because the MRI needed approval first. I proceeded to get dressed and went home.

Unfortunately, I was told it could take up to seven to ten days for approval. I was praying, considering I now had a baby's head in my thigh, that it might get pushed through a bit faster. Nope!

MARCH 19

I went back in to see Dr. Rutkowski, but this time he needed more blood-work and to write additional notes for insurance to take his request seriously.

Insurance denied his MRI request the first time. I thought maybe they needed me to actually give birth to this baby before they would actually approve it.

APRIL 3

I didn't think today would get here fast enough when I could meet Dr. Gemma. I thought for sure he would know what you are. After all, he is a surgeon, has probably seen these many times and would just cut you out. Maybe a nice little C-section, but of course, he also had no clue of what you were, so he ordered a CT scan and guess what? Yep, it was denied, but an x-ray was approved. "These people are idiots," I thought, and of course the x-ray showed nothing, just as everyone thought. About five weeks after the x-ray showed nothing, Dr Gemma put in for another MRI, like Dr. Rutkowski first did, and it was finally approved!!! Thank God because it showed a mass, at that time, of 9 cm x 5.2 cm x 2.9 cm. As I anxiously awaited the results, calling day after day after day to see what the MRI had shown, Dr. Gemma still did not think it was anything serious. When speaking to him directly on the phone, after he received the MRI results, he still thought you were a lipoma. I even asked specifically if he thought you were cancer, and he said, "no", just like the other three doctors said. "What a relief," I thought. However after Dr. Rutkowski received the MRI results the same day, approximately 30 minutes after Dr. Gemma, his office immediately called and referred me to Dr. Getty, UH Oncologist. I think Dr. Rutkowski finally knew that this small walnut was something serious after two years. Of course, now it had grown to the size of a small baby's head. Lol.

APRIL 26

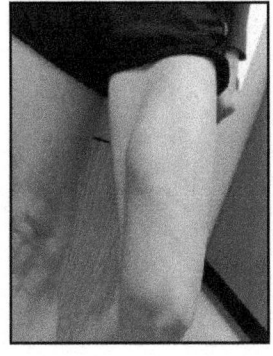

Today Beth and I met Dr. Getty for the first time. As we were waiting for him to enter, I kept thinking..."I wonder if this doctor actually knows what you are?" After all, this is the 4th doctor/surgeon who has seen you and/or reviewed my tests. I am sure he is going to say it is an Angiolipoma. Dr. Getty entered the room, and he introduced himself. He was very nice and began by looking at me and asking if he could examine you. Of course, I said yes, but to not push on you or I may hit him. Of course, I was being sarcastic, yet serious. He came up to me as I sat on the table, looked at you and then lightly touched you. I said I thought you were an Angiolipoma due to lipomas not causing pain. He looked at me with a blank look on his face, sat back in his chair and said he has looked at all of my tests, yet he to had no clue of what you were. OMG! Another doctor, this time a surgeon, the top surgeon for UH hospitals, has no clue either. How can no one know? It was that moment that I thought, "Hmmmm, you could be something serious," yet I was also thinking, "No way!" I think Dr. Getty may have an idea. However, he wanted to be safe, and I'm sure he never wants to give a patient wrong information without substantial facts and thorough testing. Dr. Getty then ordered more bloodwork and scheduled the biopsy. I wondered how long this would take for insurance to clear? Everything has been such a long process thus far. I wonder how fast you will continue to grow?

MAY 2

After calling to confirm, the biopsy was set in two days. I was notified I needed additional blood work and would not have been able to do the biopsy without it. Thank goodness I called.

How in the hell are there so many roadblocks? One after another after another.

MAY 4

Biopsy day. What are you?

Jay and I arrive at UH downtown at approximately 11:00 AM. We waited for the formalities and check in process as I am indecisive as to what exactly my feelings are right now. I actually think Jay is much more nervous than I am. The nurse finally called us to go back, I changed into a gown, laid on a bed, was asked medical history questions, then an IV was inserted to help with relaxation sedation. Once all was set, the surgeon came in, told us the actual process and a few minutes later we were on our way. They

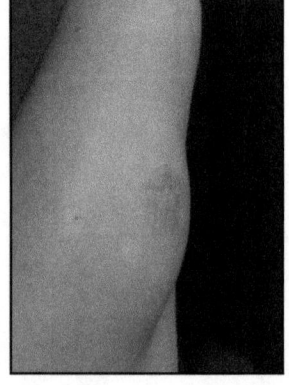

rolled me into the surgical room where I was then placed on the CT table. I looked to my right and thought, "Cool, there are the monitors. Maybe I get to actually watch?" Before the nurses prepared me for the biopsy, I told them about you, what I thought you were and how you got your name and that the birth announcement would read..., "Angie Lynn Poma" along with your measurements and weight on it. I told them that when you are taken out I would have a birthday party. They were cracking up at me. The two nurses continued to prep me while one of two surgeons spoke to me and prepared the area for the biopsy. He explained what he was going to do very thoroughly. I asked if these were the monitors that he would be using and he said yes. I asked, "Can I watch?" He said, "Not sure you want to." I said in return, "I'm not going to feel anything." So I asked him to explain what was on the monitor. He pointed out my muscle, my bone and marrow as well as your big fat head in my leg. He explained everything in detail, and he consulted with the other surgeon as he inserted the needle and extracted three samples of your nasty-ass tissue. Each time he pulled one out I heard a click, and then he moved the needles position and took another: three in total. Each piece he removed was placed into a single, sterile jar. I think the whole process maybe lasted 30 minutes. After the surgeons left, I asked the nurse if I could see the biopsies. She said, "Oh yes," and she held up the clear jar above my head. It was so weird. It looked like pieces of pink shredded cheese. They disconnected the machinery, and I went to the recovery room for about an hour. Then I got up, and we were on our way. It did not really hurt then or after. Now we wait...The next appointment with Dr. Getty is scheduled for May 10, next week, to find out the biopsies results. Well, I bet you can guess what I did every day prior to my appointment, since I was so anxious to know the outcome. Yep, I looked at my chart online. It was very nerve racking. I had to know ASAP.

MAY 9

Today, as I did the past few days, I decide to look online in anticipation of my results. To my surprise, I discovered they had my biopsy procedure notes listed along with a second note from pathology. I glanced at it quickly before lunch duty and thought, "Geeze, I wish I knew already." At least there was something listed. A bunch of notes is all." I was on pins and needles waiting for the

Results
ALICIA HANNAH

Case Surgical Pathology

FINAL DIAGNOSIS
A. LEFT THIGH
MASS, CORE
NEEDLE BIOPSY:
– MYXOID
LIPOSARCOMA.

Staff consultant: Dr.
Robin Elliott, MD

results, but did, however, have a doctor's appointment with Dr. Getty the following day, so I knew I only had one more day to wait if nothing else. I knew Geri and Tommi were anxiously awaiting the results as well. When I ran into Geri during lunch, I also had her read the notes. I don't think she thought anything of them either. After leaving the lunch room, I went into the gym, where I can have my few minutes of sanity during my day, and decided I would reread the notes, and I read them more thoroughly. It was then I discovered what I was actually reading was my diagnosis. It was there, online, and I missed it my first time reading it. I read it a third time and said to myself, "HOLY SHIT..... you have an actual name. You are called a Myxoid Liposarcoma." As I continued to read, I began to cry in the shocking way of disbelief in what I was reading. I screenshotted the diagnosis and sent it to my mother. Before I went into hysterics, I wanted to be sure you were actually what I understood you to be. She confirmed, yes you were. So I flat out asked the question, to make sure she knew the exact question I was asking, "So it is Cancer???" She said, "Yes!!!!" I sent my new devastating discovery news to Tommi and Geri where they began texting me. I was, by this time, crying uncontrollably in disbelief. How could I have cancer? Let alone a very rare form of soft tissue sarcoma? How does this happen? The fucking baby's head, whom I had already named Angie, after what I thought positively was an angiolipoma, was actually now cancer. I guess it was always cancer; I just didn't know it. Tommi came down to the gym to console me. I cried and cried and cried for about 15 minutes in disbelief. I mean how could four other doctors/surgeons think you were just a mass, lipoma, angiolipoma, cyst etc. and not have a clue you were cancer. My God, how does this happen? As I was trying to collect myself enough to continue my afternoon classes, I sent a text to Kevin, my boss at the time, letting him know of my diagnosis, but I asked him to please not come to my classroom. I thought he would only make me cry worse, and I was right. I no more hit the send button and he was in my room hugging me tightly, trying to console me. I was trying to collect myself to get through the day, but obviously that didn't work. Tommi offered to take my classes, and Kevin sent me home.

All I could think of was that everything will be ok. Today is no different than yesterday except Angie now had an actual name. Now let's do something about getting rid of her. I knew the kids would be devastated to find out the news, and they were, especially Brooke. When I returned home, all I could think about was to stay busy and keep my mind occupied, so I decided to mow the grass. While I was mowing the backyard, Brooke arrived home from her dermatologist appointment and asked why was I home so early? She is way too smart, plus I asked her to find out the last time I was at the same dermatologist for the lump. I thought for sure she wouldn't realize what time it actually was or why I was asking about the date of my last visit. When she found me in the backyard she yelled, "Hey, Mom!" and I shut the mower off. She asked, "Why are you home so early?" My response was I wasn't feeling well. She then asked, "Then why are you mowing the grass?" It was at that very moment, I looked at her and she looked directly back at me and knew. She replied, "You have cancer." I started to cry as I shook my head in affirmation as she hysterically started to cry. She walked towards me, and I held her tightly for what seemed like an eternity. I told her everything was going to be alright, that now we just have to deal with it. She was so beside herself, so afraid of me dying, she actually called her father to tell him. She did not want to leave my side for days. Later in the day, we made plans to spend the next day together before my follow up appointment. I suggested we go to lunch and get our nails done. Brooke's comment was, "Mom, you need to not spend money." I think she was afraid I would not be able to pay for my treatment, and I almost responded.... "Brooke, I can't take it with me when I go," but decided it was not a good time to be sarcastic. Lol. We enjoyed the next day together before my appointment. I did not think it was a good idea for her to go with me since I wanted to be able to focus on the information Dr. Getty was going to give me and my treatment plan to come.

MAY 10

Today was my follow up with Dr. Getty. Kathy went with me for moral support and for an extra pair of ears, so I would totally understand what he was saying and how we would proceed with my plan of treatment. In a way, I was devastated to find out the diagnosis online, but I do believe it allowed me to be 100% coherent in my questions and understanding the feedback Dr. Getty was giving me. As we were waiting for Dr. Getty to enter, an intern pathologist entered the room. I think he thought he was going to break the news gently to me before Dr. Getty entered, but I told him I knew my diagnosis. He commented, "Okay then, let me go get Dr. Getty." A few minutes later Dr. Getty came in and said, "So you already know." I said, "Yes, I found out online." We discussed for quite a while what exactly you were, what the severity was and what my treatment plan would be. Kathy, I think, was more worried about you than I was. Kathy asked Dr. Getty how rare you are? Dr. Getty confirmed he does not see a lot of cancers such as you, but if anyone was the person to get rid of you, he was the man to do so. Dr. Getty then said to us, "There are unicorns and zebras. Unicorns are those people whose cancer you know they will not survive from. The zebras are people whose cancer is treatable". He looked right at me and said, "You are not a unicorn." I gave him a high five and we cheered. He discussed with us the treatment plan of additional MRI and a CT scan to make sure you had not spread, 25 radiation treatments, resection surgery and then a continued lifelong series of tests which would be every four months for the first two years, every six months for two years and then every year for life. He said we are going to have a relationship for life. Before leaving, Dr. Getty ordered CT scans of my chest and abdomen to make sure you had not metastasized. He then referred me to Dr. Mansur for radiology treatment and to receive those results. He told me he would see me five to six weeks after my last radiation treatment.

MAY 12

Tonight was the first real time, since you were growing inside me, I feared you could actually take over my life. You always hear of animals knowing when someone is ill, but I had never really experienced it first hand. Not only did Toby seem very aware of my situation, apparently Turbo, Karen's cat, did as well. As I lie on her couch watching movies, Turbo, who NEVER goes to strangers, jumped up on the couch, climbed on top of my leg and laid his head directly on you. I think Karen and Jeff, her husband, were in shock. As I started to pet Turbo and lay my hand underneath his head so he would not put pressure on

you, an overwhelming feeling of death rose over me. I felt an empty pit and a hot burning sensation in my stomach. I thought I was going to pee my pants, I was so scared that you would be the reason my life was taken. My eyes began to tear in fear, but I did not let anyone see me. I thought this could be it, and there is absolutely nothing I can do about it! Once again, after a few deep breaths, I put you out of my mind and concentrated on staying busy and prayed for the CT scan to come back cleared.

MAY 15

I am so happy today. I met Dr. Mansur and he confirmed you were, in fact, localized in my thigh. Thank God! Now you didn't seem so serious to me. In the back of my mind I thought, "So does that mean you are only half cancer or still cancer?" Lol! We discussed radiation treatment, and he was comfortable with Dr. Katcher taking my case at Southwest Seidman Center. Twenty-five treatments for five weeks, every day, except weekends. Oh boy…fun to come!

MAY 21

I met Dr. Katcher, and Anaida, his nurse, had my mold created for treatment and was prepped for radiation. It was so weird when I went in to make the mold. The girls had me hop on the table, insert my left leg into a huge plastic bean bag like apparatus, and blew air in it so it would become hard as a rock. They took a bunch of measurements, drew a road map of pink marks, where treatment would be lined up on, covered them with clear stickers and pro-grammed the machine for my specific treatment information. It was pretty cool, I do have to say. Today Dr. Katcher also discussed with me the side effects of radiation. He said the area would become very red and irritated like a deep sunburn and possibly blister along with possible fatigue. God, I can't wait. Lol. We do what we gotta do. Better than the alternative for sure.

RADIATION PREP

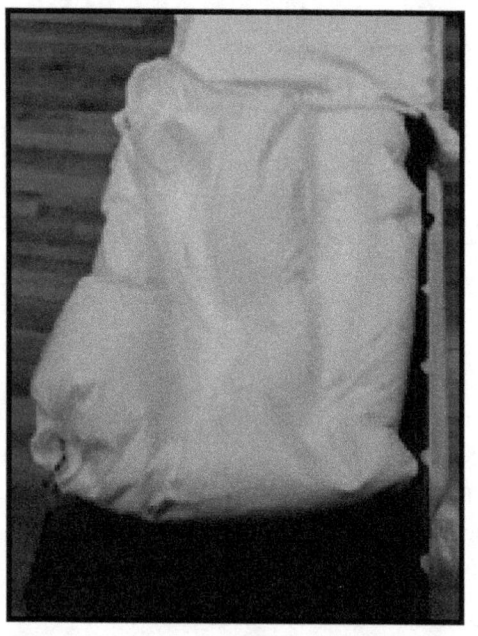
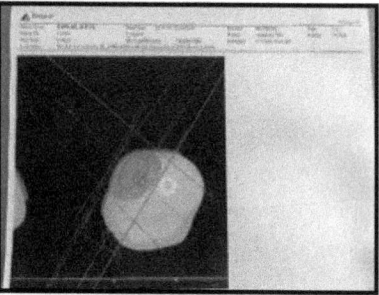
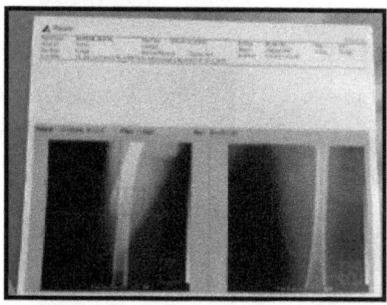
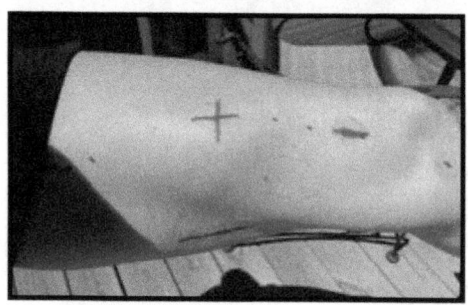
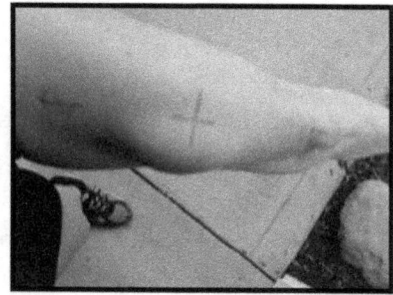

MAY 24

My last prep appointment and test run before treatments start on May 29. As I sit waiting for my appointment to begin, I can't help wondering how all this is about to affect my life. I wonder how I will feel, how my skin will change, how my daily activities will differ. I am again nervous and a bit anxious of what today entails. Will I get to finally remove the pink marks I've been sporting around for four days? As I was waiting to go back for my "final fitting", I heard a voice call my name. It was Hilary. She is one of the staff whom I met this past Monday. She took me back, introduced me to three other staffers who would be helping, gave me a little tour of where the monitors are, showed me the computer where the radiation gets programed from and had me enter the room in which I would be getting my treatments. Once I was situated, they had me lay down on the treatment table and insert my legs into my special premade mold. They began looking at table measurements, calling numbers out and putting information into the computer. Once all was in and the radiation machine was positioned properly, they would all leave the room while it scanned in specific dimensions for my treatments. This happened four or five times and the machine was positioned at different angles. They must radiate through all angles and sides of you without hitting my bone.

MAY 28

Today is Memorial Day, a reflection day and THE day before I am to start my long journey of treatments. Lucky number 25 to be exact, Dr. Katcher tells me. As I sit anxiously awaiting tomorrow, I can't help wondering still if this is real? How in the F_ _ _ did I end up with cancer, let alone a rare kind? Dr. Getty says I'm a zebra and not a unicorn, but maybe I am a unicorn after all? I ponder what is the lesson I am supposed to learn from this life altering experience? I wonder how hard the next 16 weeks will be until you are out of me, and I am finally, completely rid of you and healed? All I know right now is that you better hang on because I am about to kick your ass and throw you out!!!!

MAY 29

Treatment #1

I arrived at the center a few minutes early, and I sat in anticipation of my name being called. However, a nurse comes out and calls another's name and she says, "Yes?" The nurse proceeds to say out loud, "You know what today is? You are going to ring that bell!!!" The nurse offered to push her back in her wheelchair and the woman stands up out of her wheelchair and says, "I'm not going back my last day in that chair." I gave her a cheer and a little clap, and she was on her way. After her treatment the nurse came into the waiting room to get her husband. I thought, "OMG, it's about to happen for her. She has finished her long journey of radiation, and finally she will get to ring that infamous bell I have been hearing about." I wanted to almost cry for joy for her as I heard that bell ding three very slow, but loud, dings. I thought to myself, "On July 2, 2018, that WILL be me!!!" As I passed her on my way in for my first treatment, I said to her, "Congratulations. You are finished, and I am just beginning," and we smiled at each other. As I entered the treatment room, I was greeted by a few new faces. "There are so many," I thought. However, Hilary is the only one who has been there each time so far. I jumped up on the table, inserted my legs into my mold and the numbers started flying. They were checking angles before proceeding with treatment. After everything was checked for accuracy, Irene placed a warm soft jelly molded apparatus on my leg and matched it up with the blue lines and taped it down. "This is called a bolus," she said. When I asked what it was for she answered, "To keep the radiation towards the surface of the skin." Once all was in place and lined up, the treatment began. All I had to do was lay still, listen to the music and look at the beautiful scenic picture that was portrayed from the lights above. The machine moved three different times and let out two high pitched tones each time. The first two being longer than the last. Once the machine moved three times, the nurse said, "Ok, we are all done." I truly did not feel a thing. The whole treatment took about 20 minutes. I left thinking, "Ok cool...only 24 more to go!"

RADIATION TREATMENT

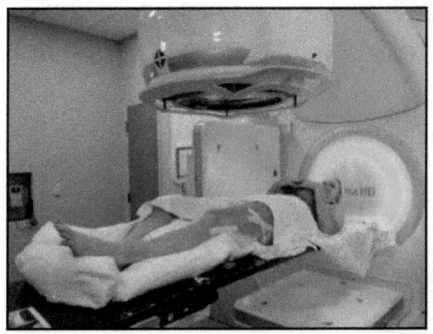 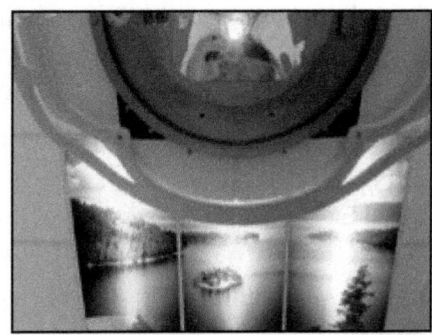

 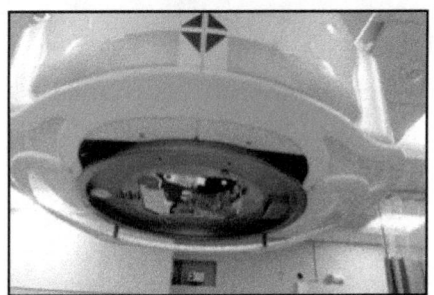

MAY 30
Day 2...23 to go!
Feeling great! No visible marks yet.

Today's treatment went faster. Found out my treatment doses. Total after 25 sessions will be 5000 cgy, daily dose 200 cgy and daily energy used is 6 mv and 10 mv. The bolus on top of my skin acts like another layer of skin to help protect the surface from the intense radiation because the tumor is shallow toward the surface. After radiation, my skin feels a bit tingly. I will begin using Aquaphor tonight. I have no pain. I continued my regular workout and mowed the grass after the sun went down. Reminded me of a vampire. Lol.

MAY 31
Day 3
I'm still feeling great. It almost seems as though you might be getting a tad smaller. Was it true, my imagination or wishful thinking? After all the radiation lines were now a bit off center. Could you actually change that quickly? I thought, "Angie, you have no chance in hell now!!!!" 22 to go!

JUNE 1
Day 4
You are responding well. Treatment continues to go well and now getting quicker!

JUNE 2 AND 3
Weekend. Woohoo! No treatments. Felt like I was getting out of school for snow days!!!!!

JUNE 3, SUNDAY
Today we spent the day at the cottage with Jay's family celebrating his birthday. Chilly and breezy but nonetheless a nice day. Angie, of course you were the talk of the day. I told the story to many of how you came to be and what the plan was to get rid of you. As we sat by the fire in the evening, I was asked more questions and I showed pictures of my journey thus far. When I was done, Scott asked if I would mind if they said a prayer for me. I was very honored. Scott, Sue, Diane and Craig all placed their hands on me, Sue on You, as I placed mine on them. They each took turns saying prayers. I was very touched and thought I was going to cry for a moment.

JUNE 4, MONDAY
Day 5, my lucky number.
Treatment went well and getting quicker. No visible signs of changing on skin's surface. Seems to be shrinking a tiny bit more.

JUNE 5
Day 6

Today went well. Took pics in addition to treatment. No visible signs of changing on skin's surface.

JUNE 6
Day 7

Feeling a bit tired today and you are a bit more sensitive to the touch. Treatment went well and pretty quick. I brought the staff some cookies. They are so nice there. I met with Dr. Katcher to check in. He looked at you and said you look good. He felt you to make sure you were not hot to the touch, and he said I am going to do fine with all the treatments. He predicts the 2nd to 3rd week you will be inflamed and red. It was a brief check in and nothing really to speak about. I will see him again next Wednesday!

Friday, Briana and Brooke are coming with me for all of the excitement. It is one thing to show people pictures and tell them my experience, but it is totally different when they get to see first hand. They can fill me in on their experience outside the treatment room while I'm in it.

JUNE 7
Day 8

Treatment went well and quickly today!

Starting to become a bit more surface sensitive and skin seems a bit pinker and puffier.

17 more to go!

JUNE 8
Day 9

Today was definitely different. Briana and Brooke came to see how they are slowly killing you. The girls gave them the grand tour and the info on how the whole radiation process works from setup to finish. They got to see first hand plus ask any questions if they wanted to. They even got to feel the bolus used on top of my thigh during treatment.

Later that evening, Jay and I went to his son-in-law's surprise birthday party at a Mexican restaurant. When we arrived at Chris' birthday party, it was a bit strange. I did not know who knew about you and who didn't know, but after awhile I figured if they knew they would ask how things were going, and if they didn't then they probably didn't know. I really do enjoy telling my story/journey to others. It makes me feel that I have valuable information that I can share and enlighten someone else. The questions were general to much more specific. I even shared my whole story to a few who knew nothing of you.

JUNE 9 AND 10

Weekend. No treatments. More snow days!!!!

JUNE 11, MONDAY

Day 10

Feeling pretty tired the last few days. I think fatigue is starting. Going to just keep life as normal as possible. I need to workout. I have been slacking. I will go slow and steady.

Treatment was quick today. Aquaphor here we come!

You are looking quite smaller!!! Pretty soon you will only be a memory.

JUNE 12

Day 11

Treatment was short and sweet. Picture day!

JUNE 13

Day 12

Treatment was short. I took a two hour nap after returning from radiation. Going well. Surface sensitivity.

JUNE 14
Lucky number 13!
More than half way and Flag Day!!!!!!
Treatment was short. I met with Dr. Katcher and Anaida to see how things are going.

A bit more fatigued. Nap time. Glad it's summer.

Redness is starting to be a bit more noticeable and little sensitive to touch. Going great!

JUNE 15
Day 14
Treatment was quick. Another nap.

Skin still looking pretty good.

JUNE 16 AND 17
Weekend. No treatments.

JUNE 18, MONDAY
Day 15
Treatment was pretty quick. Skin is a bit pinker. All is well.

JUNE 19
Day 16
OMG, I'm so excited. I feel like I can see the end! Now into single digits.

Tommi came with me so she could see what it was like. I think she was really surprised how quick it went. They actually took pics today so the appointment was a bit longer than normal.

I can tell my skin is becoming redder, but still in great shape.

Keep applying Aquaphor!!

JUNE 20
Day 17
Short and sweet. Skin looks pretty good still and no fatigue.

JUNE 21
Day 18
Short and sweet. Skin looks pretty good still and no fatigue.

JUNE 22
Day 19
Short and sweet. Skin looks pretty good still and no fatigue.

You are almost just a memory now, other than the marker road map I still have. Lol.

JUNE 23 AND 24
Weekend. No treatments.

JUNE 25, MONDAY
Day 20
Brooke and Patrick went with me. It was very quick. I met with Doctor Katcher. All is going well. He still seems to think the redness is still going to come even more. Right now it's not bad at all.

A bit itchy at times, but not bad at all.

Lucky number five to go!!!

JUNE 26
Day 21
Short and sweet. Picture day.

JUNE 27
Day 22

Short and sweet. Red and itchy.

JUNE 28
Day 23

Short and sweet. Red and itchy. Prickly feeling. OMG, only two more days. So excited!

JUNE 29
Day 24

In a funny kind of way, I am a bit sad this will be my last day I see a few of the girls. They have been so sweet and always answered my questions and kept me informed. I will go back and see them for sure after surgery. I took our picture in front of the fountain, so I can add them to my scrapbook. I will get the other few Monday before I leave.

RADIATION STAFF

JUNE 30 AND JULY 1

Weekend, no treatments.

JULY 2
DAY 25
Finally, BELL DAY!!!!

I woke up this morning so excited!!!! The final day is here. I wanted to pick the right outfit to celebrate this glorious day. I woke with such excitement because I could share it with all my closest work friends. Unfortunately, Johnathon couldn't be with me. I could not wait to take and send him pictures. After getting dressed and leaving the house, the drive seemed even longer than normal. I knew Tommi and Beth were waiting at the center to watch and help me celebrate. It meant so much that they were there with me along with Brooke and Jay. It was going to be a moment that I would never forget as long as I live. I couldn't wait to walk in, kick my shoes off, say, "Yes that's me, August 1, 1967," one last time! After  treatment, I spoke to Anaida and Dr. Katcher to sum up my final day. Once all was finished, I jumped off the table and walked into the lobby and grabbed everyone. OMG! I thought I was going to bust. I took pictures first with Dr. Katcher and Anaida. After they stepped out of the way, it was time. I held that rope tightly, made sure everyone was ready with cameras and video and gave that bell a good shake. When I was done, I couldn't believe it, I became very emotional and started to cry. Brooke walked to me, we held each other, and she was bawling as well. The whole group was either crying or in awe of the moment. They all clapped. As Brooke and I continued our special moment, I asked her if she wanted to ring it with me. I held her hand on the rope and once again we rang that bell, but this time together!! I think it was the best moment of my life thus far. Once finished I took a few more pictures with Brooke and Jay, and we were off to the restaurant, El Tequila, to celebrate the glorious ending to my new beginning. The reservation was for 11:30 AM, and we were the first to arrive. They had an area with multiple tables pushed together as well as a few more beside it. I thought, "OMG! There are a lot of people going to be here to help me celebrate this glorious day." I felt so humbled and loved. We had a great lunch and were so happy that the first phase of your disappearance was over. Bring on eviction day!!!

JULY 4

Day 2 after treatment

Doing pretty well. A bit more red and itchy, but tolerable. However, I can feel you when I sleep where the pillow lays between my knees. Sometimes you awaken me. Very irritating.

JULY 6
Day 4 after treatment
Leg doing pretty well. Looks like a sunburn with tiny red marks and age spots. Oh boy!!!!

I can feel you inside pushing on occasion. I can't really bend my knee too much and sit because you pull and cause pain. Your better not be coming back!

JULY 10
Day 8 after treatment
Went for additional blood work before final MRI and CT scan scheduled for July 24, 2018.

Leg is looking very good. A bit red and very prickly looking with minor itching, but doing great.

JULY 12-16
We are Florida bound. Now the real challenge is going to be how do I camouflage your ass from the sun and people staring at you. You are like a Gremlin: you can't see the sun and I'm not allowed to get you wet. Thank goodness for my pretty matching purple sarong wrap. It worked perfectly to cover your ugly ass up.

JULY 16-20
You are a bit more irritating each day. Itchy, red and stingy. When I run my fingers lightly over you, after feeling like digging my nails into you, you feel like a prickly rash almost like a terrible heat rash. Trying to take daily pictures to see your healing progression, or not.

I am meeting with Dr. Getty on Thursday; I am praying he is ok with your progress and we forge ahead with your eviction date, August 15, 2018. Keeping up with the ice!!!!

JULY 21
Day 19 after treatment
Angie, you are still a nuisance!!!

Red, itchy and stinging. You keep me from sleeping at times and make me want to scratch you like a case of terrible poison ivy. God, I can't wait until you are gone. Thank goodness for ice bags.

JULY 22
Day 20 after treatment
OMFG! You need to go!!!!

You are red, itchy, raw, irritating, and I want to pull my hair out. The only thing that seems to give me relief from you is coolness. At times it feels like every nerve on top of my thigh is tickling me, making me want to dig into the surface of my skin. Everything that touches you feels like cat claws scraping. I try not to let my shorts touch you even. I pray this is the worst day because I'm not sure I can take it much longer. Almost like the worst case of poison ivy ever!!! Not fun at all. Booo!!!

AFTER RADIATION TREATMENT

Day 5   Day 8   Day 10   Day 12

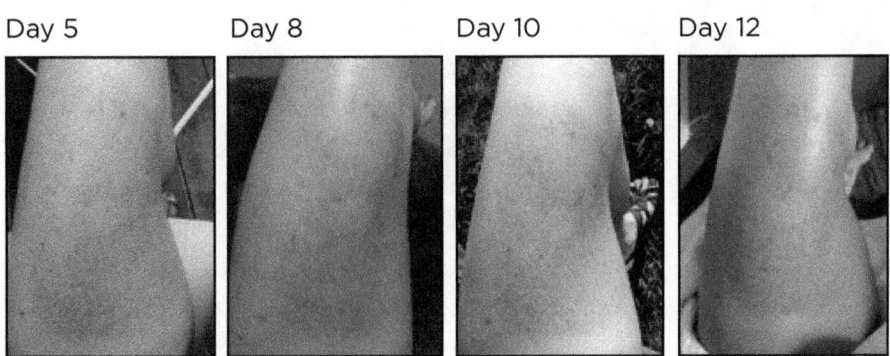

Day 15   Day 18 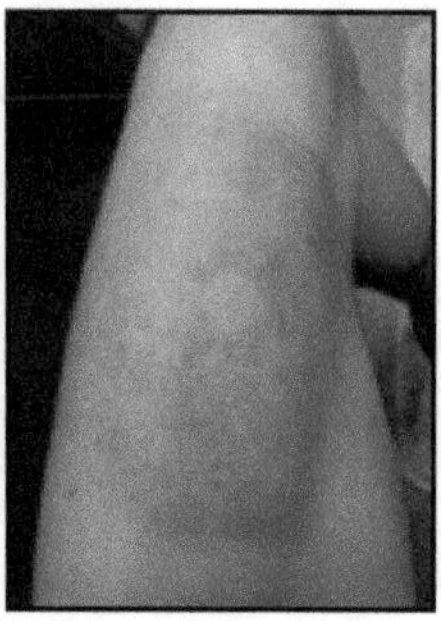   Day 21 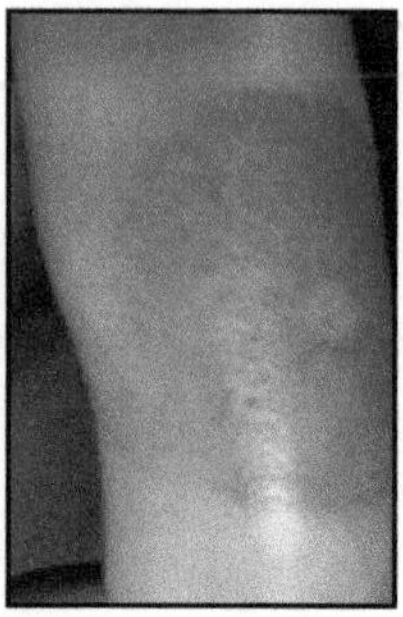   Day 25

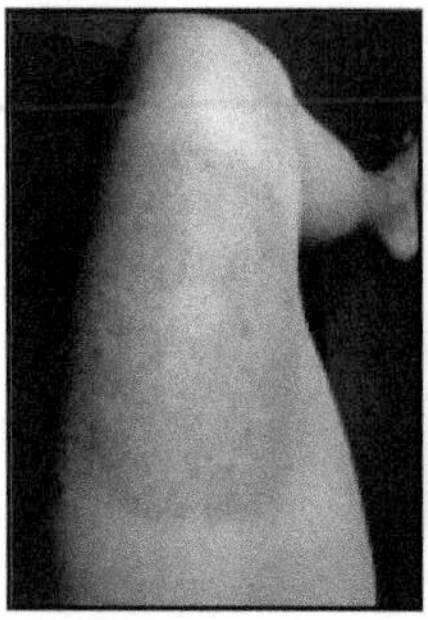

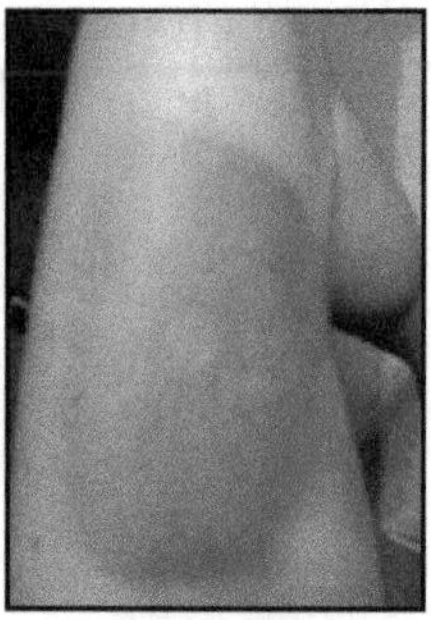

Day 29 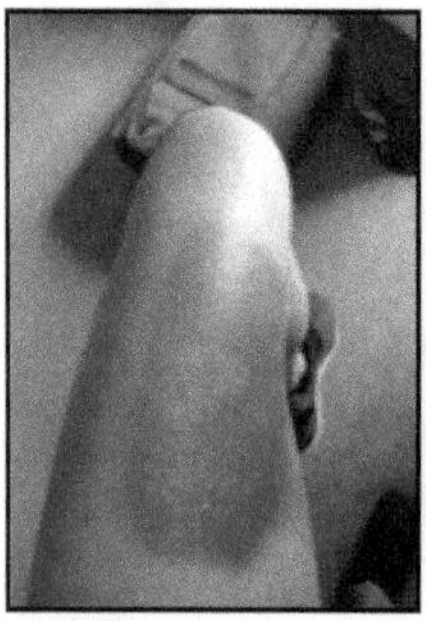   Day 30 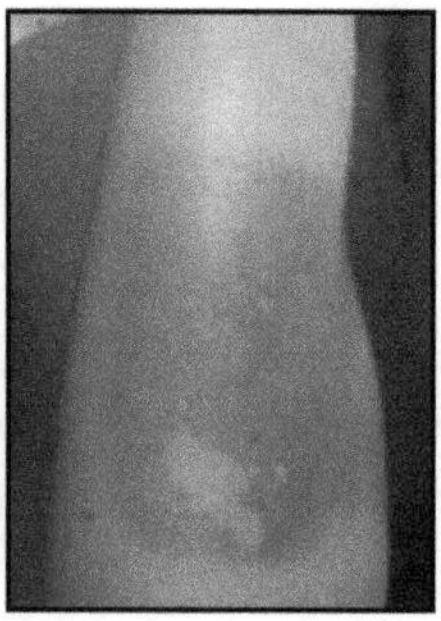   Day 33 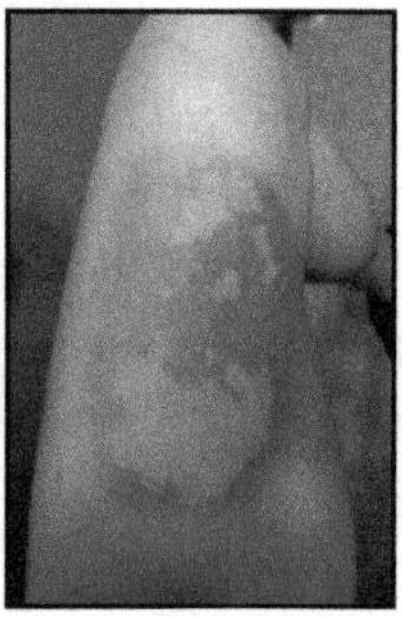   Day 36

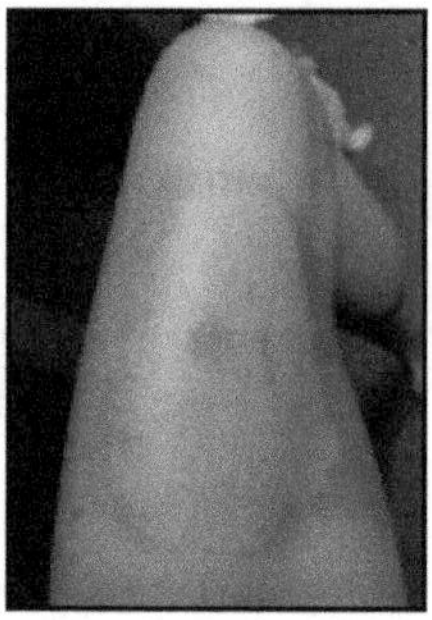

Day 42

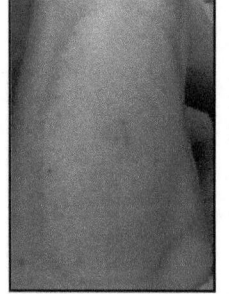

JULY 24

A big day today. It's my follow up MRI and CT scan after radiation to see if you are still cleared from other areas or are you still hanging around? Be gone already! The results will be discussed with Dr. Getty soon. However, today you are still a pain in my ass. I can't even have anything brush against my leg without it feeling like severe cat scratches. OMFG! You hurt and you continue to itch like the worst case of poison ivy ever. Are you going to be healed by eviction day? I wonder what Dr. Getty is going to say Thursday? Will he move the date? It took three hours to complete the CT scan and MRI today. You itched so badly during that 1:15 minute scan that I wanted to explode. I had to hold perfectly still, not even a flinch or a scratch at all during that time. You have been trying my patience a great deal lately. You might be the thing that actually drives me crazy!!!! I guess it's safe to say yesterday wasn't the worst day because today is just as bad. Let's see what tomorrow has in store for us...

JULY 25
Day 23 after treatment
Give me a break already!!!!

Red, raw, itchy, bruised, painful and irritating.

JULY 26
My appointment is at 1:15 PM with Dr. Getty to discuss the results and prep for surgery. Skin is so irritated I wonder if he is going to suggest pushing back surgery date?? Beth and Kathy went with me to the appointment for moral support, and well, today was a bit of a shock. You were nowhere to be seen on the MRI! Although it was great news, you have now made your eviction more of a challenge for Dr. Getty. Dr. Getty has now decided that he will use your original measurements in your removal along with margin. He is going to open you up in an ecliptic form, take pieces, send tissue samples to pathology until the entire area is cleared. Then he will turn the procedure over to Dr. Long where he will continue with skin grafting to close the area up. According to Dr. Getty, there is not a lot of fat in the area so he foresees going wide and down to the fascia and taking a bit of my muscle. I will be in the recovery care of Dr. Long after surgery until I am totally healed, and then the continued care of Dr. Getty. Dr. Getty is predicting a four hour surgical time and, at least, an eight to twelve week recovery period. As of today, Dr. Getty feels that you are too irritated from radiation to complete surgery, but is optimistic. Once I meet with Dr. Long, and again with Dr. Getty on Aug 10, together they will determine whether surgery is a go for August 15. Looks like there will be walker races with mom!!!! Can't I be done with you already? You are throwing me another curve ball. My thigh is going to look beautiful. Lol. I'm requesting a butt lift for my grafting area.

JULY 28
Day 26 after treatment

I actually think my skin is on the mend!!!! Darker in tone, a bit purple and definitely not as red or irritated, but still pretty itchy at times. I'm getting my hopes up for Eviction Day!!!!

I want this done and over with. I was thinking today of all the experiences I will have or want to have while recovering. Letting Mom take care of me like she did when I was little, while Dad cooks us dinner, then cleans up the kitchen. I can visualize it all now. Me lying around doing absolutely nothing...yeah, like that's going to actually happen. I'll have to sneak a few sit ups in when Mom is not looking. I want to have walker races with Mom and videotape them for Facebook. I want to ride in a cart in the grocery store and listen to that loud annoying beep as I go in reverse and play hide and seek with Mom while she finds my orange flag. Lastly, I want to see all my friends stop by and envy that they are not me all bandaged up, just to name a few. It is going to be quite the experience!

AUG. 1
Today is my birthday!! 51!

My leg is looking great! Redness is pretty much gone; however, it is still itchy at times but the skin is turning brown and starting to heal. It's starting to look like Michael Jackson's face. Lol.

Where the skin is peeling, healthy skin is being exposed. I'm so excited. I think August 15th will actually be eviction day after all.

AUG. 2 THRU 4
New Orleans

OMG, so many memories...I can't speak of the details, but they are embedded in my brain. What happens in New Orleans stays in New Orleans. I will never forget our balcony memories, Dawn's big beads, the awesome dancing and the gummy bears...Geri. Great times!!!!

AUG. 6

The peeling is much better. Not exactly sure why you are causing me cramping and pain again if you are dead. Are you actually dead or are you just dormant? I've been feeling very nervous and anxious lately. I just want to get this done so life can get back to normal, if that will ever actually happen again? I keep running things in my mind of how I think recovery will actually be and curious as to how much will be correct. Praying Aug. 15th is a go!

AUG. 10

Today I got the news that your ASS is out of here from both Dr. Long and Dr. Getty!!!

Tommi arrived at 7:30 AM for our departure to hopefully, as I was praying, confirm your eviction day, another date I have been waiting so long for. I can't believe how my skin has healed in just a few short weeks since I had seen Dr. Getty last. I don't think either of us thought you would look so good. Today you are more like a big, leathering, rough feeling, lighter patch with tanned skin still surrounding you, like an old hag now and not a baby's head.

We started at Dr. Long's office for our first appointment. As we waited for him to arrive, we decided to look up his info. We were shocked. His picture looked like he was about 16 years old.

He arrived at the office as we were called back, and Tommi and I both thought, "Ok, maybe he isn't so young after all." Don't get me wrong, he looked young, early 30s I'd say. He was very pleasant and discussed with me the three procedures he was considering after taking over from Dr. Getty, like a tag team, provided his schedule was clear. He was up for the challenge. Now we were off to see Dr. Getty. So the two of us became three. Like the three amigos, Beth joined us. We arrived at Dr. Getty's a bit early, and they took us back pretty quickly, then we waited and waited and waited. It seemed like forever. I wanted to get on with it. I wanted to know if the date was actually going to be in stone. Dr. Getty came in very happy and smiling. He just got back from vacation, but I want to think it was because he took one look at your nasty ass and was shocked how my skin had healed so well in such a short time. He confirmed that all looked great, and since Dr. Long was right on board, Aug. 15th at 9:00 AM was a go! I got the living room all set up and ready for recovery. God, I can't wait!!!

AUG. 13

Two days before eviction day and all is going well. Dr. Long called to give me a heads up that there is a small chance that he may not be able to do his magic on Wednesday due to another case right before mine. If he cannot, he will complete it the following Monday or Wednesday. He wants to do a skin flapping procedure which takes longer and is more intricate than grafting. He doesn't want to rush perfection! I am of course hoping that both can be done the same day, but if it can't, then I agree with him totally.

AUG. 14

One more day until eviction day. I am ready and have complete faith in Dr. Getty and Dr. Long. I have left nothing unturned or unspoken in my personal life. My finances are in order, and the letters to Brooke and Johnathon have been written. Lets go!

It's so weird, Tommi asked how I was doing today. Surprisingly, I don't feel any different today than any other day; I am very calm. This evening, however, I was a bit more anxious when Mom and Jay got here. I just need to make sure I have everything for my five star hotel stay.

AUG. 15
Eviction Day!!!!!!!!!!!!!
DAY OF SURGERY

Autopsy day for Angie is here, and then the results in seven to ten days with Dr. Getty.

So, of course, I did not get much sleep last night. I just want to know why I woke up singing "Chameleon" by Boy George? LMAO

I will be waking the crew in a few minutes and leaving at 6:15 AM sharp. At least, I will be asleep all day because I only slept for a few hours last night. Boy, was I mistaken. Lol.

So we arrived at the hospital by 7:00 AM for my 9:00 AM surgery. I checked in and was told it had been moved to 12:00 PM. Grrrr. We were given a pager, kind of like the ones in a restaurant, and we waited. We went into waiting room where I found a little comfy area where I could rest. I no
more than laid down for about 10 minutes, and they called my name. I jumped up and said, "Really?" Then quietly shouted, "Let's get this party started." The receptionist walked me to the operating room entrance where I was greeted by a nurse who had me change and pee in a cup. I came out of the restroom and a man, who looked like a doctor, said "I'll take that for you." I said, "Cool, thanks." They proceeded to take me into a small room sectioned off by a curtain. They were like small stalls all lined up on both sides of the hallway, kind of like cattle. Various people stopped in asking many questions and logging information. Pretty soon Dr. Wallace, my anesthesiologist, came in and introduced himself, but I already knew who he was. I said, "Thanks for taking my pee earlier!" He chuckled and said that they were full service facility. He made me laugh. After I got my new stylish stocking on my right leg, a resident came in and wrote his name on the spot where Angie was to be removed. Dr. Long stopped in to say hello and told me about another option he might use. Pig skin, but he called it something else. I told him whatever would make it look the best was the one I was picking, and that I trusted him 100%. After a while, Mom and Jay came in for one last goodbye before I went off to surgery. A few moments later, I was whisked off to surgery, and then woke up with someone saying, "Alicia, all done." They took me to my room to start my recovery

process. It was then that I realized I could no longer call you Angie. The area, now covered, that had been operated on was now just my leg with a hole in it, sewn shut with a drain, and a seal vacuum on it all wrapped up from my upper thigh area to my toes. As I sat speaking to Mom and Jay, Dr. Getty stopped by to explain what he had done and to check on me. Dr. Getty conveyed he removed an elliptical segment of skin with subcutaneous tissue measuring 17.2 cm x 5.2 cm x 1.8 cm and revealed an 8.2 cm x 2.2 cm x 1.6 cm circumscribed tan-pink myxoid nodule. OMG!

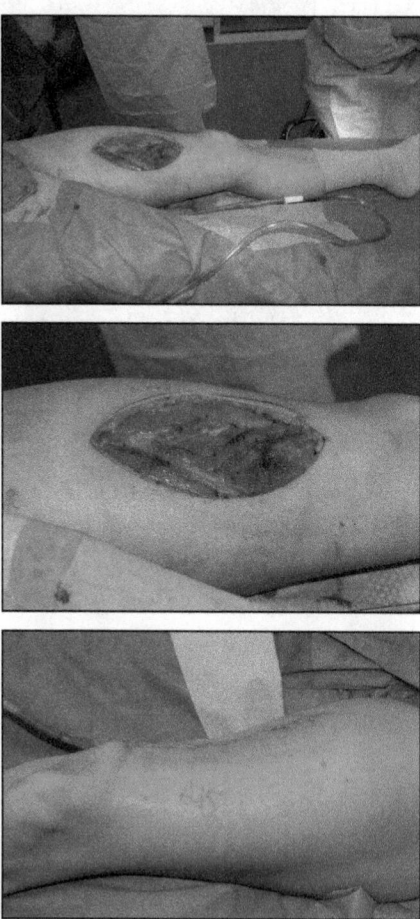

Photos by Dr. Long

Later in the evening Tommi, Beth and Crystal stopped by to see how I was doing and to say hello. Tommi and Beth came in with a huge helium balloon and flowers. It was so nice to see them and Crystal. Shortly after they left, Mom and Jay left, so I could rest. I 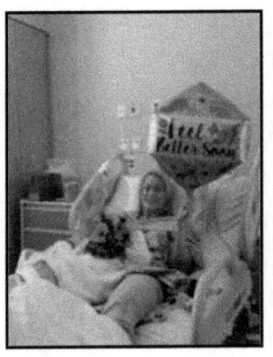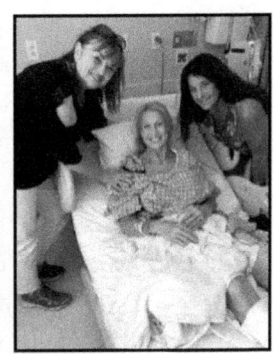 had good intentions, but there was no resting involved. Lol.

AUG. 16

OMG, I am a zombie! Of course, I got no sleep. All I kept thinking is that I want to unplug the stinking pump feeding me my meds. Between people waking me to check my vitals, to the drip makings noises, the pump slurping, and having to pee, I got absolutely no sleep. By the time 3:00 AM rolled around, I even went as far as peeing in a cup that was sitting on my table. I figured there was no way I am calling anyone else into my room, so I scoped out the area and thought, "How am I going to pee by myself?" I thought, "OMG, I can grab the cup, a washcloth off the table, balance on my good knee, and relieve myself." That is exactly what I did. I was so proud of myself and relieved, literally. When the nurse came in the next morning, I told him what was in the cup, and I thought he was going to faint. He could not believe I actually did it! I was a woman on a mission. Morning came and I decided to finally eat. Runny cream of wheat and half wheat bagel, not good, but at least better than the liquid diet with nasty jello I had the night before. Not sure how you make jello taste nasty but UH did. Lol.

The morning became busier and busier with doctors, nurses, PT, OT and God only knows who else. All of them working to get me discharged. At this point, I gave up even trying to sleep. I watched *Naked and Afraid* and waited for Mom to arrive. We were out of there by 2:00 PM and home on the couch by 3:00 PM exhausted. I knew by the time I got on the couch, (Mom and Jay were in the room with me, then Johnathon and his girlfriend came in) that there was no way

I was going to be able to sleep on the couch. I thought I needed to somehow get up those stairs. So I strategized and ended up pulling myself up the stairs backwards, good tricep workout, and I slept in my own bed. I was in heaven. Ahhhh!

AUG. 17

Two days after surgery I am feeling tired and restless. I spent most of the day on the couch watching movies. I am not a fan of sitting still, I might add. Mom has been hanging with me, making me food and taking care of me. Mom asked what I would like for lunch? I said, "I think peanut butter and banana sandwich with peanut butter on both sides please." She had put so much peanut butter on it that it got stuck in my throat. Lol. She wanted to make sure she made it really good for me, so she took some off.

Later in the evening, I had a few visitors: Karen, Elisa and Amy. Karen brought a little care package for me to keep busy. She is an awesome friend. I am so lucky. My PT, Nikki came by and showed me a few exercises to do to start strengthening my leg. She will come out one time each week. She was surprised at how well I was already getting around.

AUG. 18

Three days after eviction day, and I am feeling pretty good. There is pain every now and again but not that bad at all. I am resting and keeping my leg elevated. Movie marathon days!!!! The couch may have indents by the time I can start moving around more. I already think my back is the shape of the couch. Annoying.

AUG. 19

OMG, how many movies can I watch? Lol, I may lose my mind. At least they are decent ones, and ones I had not yet seen. Mom keeps picking and I keep saying that I saw that one, saw that one, and saw that one too. All those elliptical hours of movies were coming back to hinder my recovery distractions.

I continue to keep my food intake in check so I don't gain. You know, at my age it's harder to take off later. Shhh... don't tell Mom, but I peeked under the wrap to see my wound vac. OMG, it is so long. All I can think of is how long is my scar going to actually be? WOW! It is definitely going to be a conversation piece for sure. Lol, war wound.

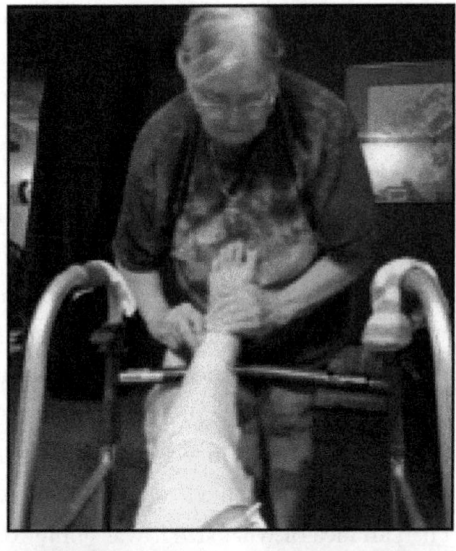

AUG. 20

Same old. I am feeling pretty good. The movie marathon continues. The annoying areas are my foot arch, back of my knee and the inner thigh where vac and wrap are placed. I have no idea what Dr. Long will say. I can't wait.

AUG. 21

Today is my follow up with Dr. Long. I wonder what he will do today? Will the drain and vac come off? How badly is this going to hurt? Beth is

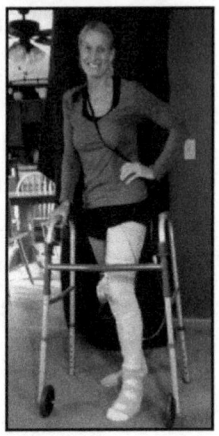

meeting Mom and I. I am glad she comes along for the ride. She is a good friend.

So I pretty much did not sleep and finally got up at 5:00 AM. There is terrible pinching and stinging, burning pain that periodically runs down the inside of my thigh. It takes my breath away. I almost cried, such burning. It's only 7:15 AM. I hope the day gets better!?

Well, the day was another adventure in this relatively short journey in life. I was in such wonder as to what Dr. Long would do or say. When we arrived at the office, we were taken back after a brief wait. Tiera showed us into an exam room, told me to hop on the table, and proceeded to take my wrap off. It felt like a tight sock you couldn't wait to get off your ankle and scratch like crazy after five long days. It was such a relief. I was in such suspense; I could not wait to see what my wound vac and my drain looked like. She started to pull back the tape on the edges of the vac., some parts hurt like a very sticky bandage was applied, and yet, some areas were totally numb and I could not feel anything. That seemed a bit concerning, even though Dr. Getty said it would be that way for quite a while, possibly even years. As the tape loosened, the vac's suction loosened and the sponge became full again. She pulled up the sponge and for the first time I could see what seemed like a huge purple road map down my thigh. I had an idea of what size it was going to be, but to actually finally see it, in real life, scared me a bit. I thought, "Now this is going to be a conversation piece for the rest of my life. Very cool!!!" I can only imagine what it would have looked like if I would have needed grafting. Once the sponge was pulled back, it was connected to the drainage hole and the drain valve. At this time, Tiera went to get Dr. Long. After discussing how much drainage there was the last few days, he gave the go ahead and decided to remove the tube. As he was preparing to remove the tube, he looked at me and said, "Okay, are you ready? Take a deep breath." He then pulled a seven inch tube out of a hole underneath the area of the incision.

DAY OF THE REVEALING - DR. LONG

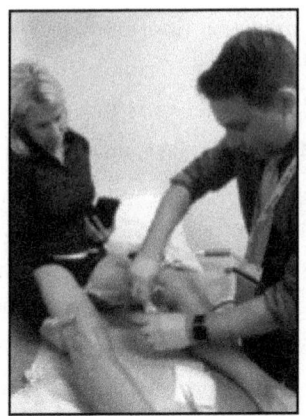 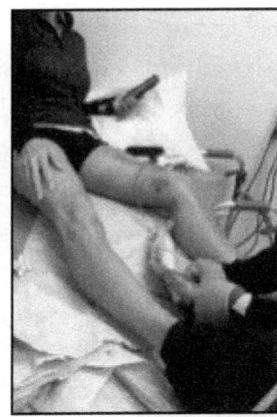

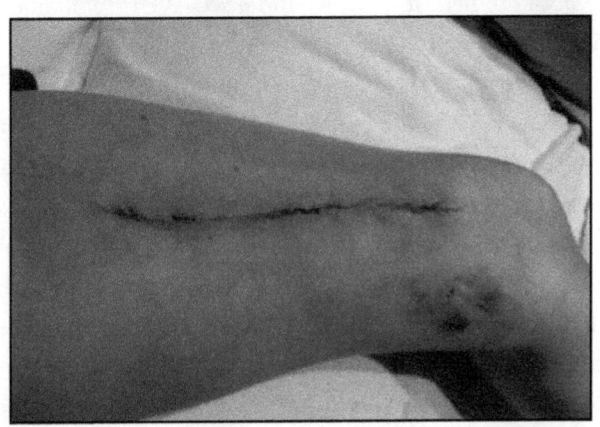

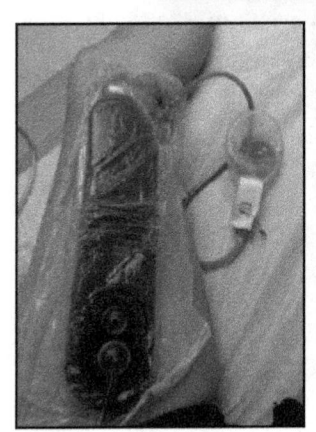 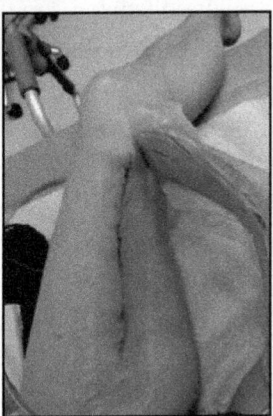 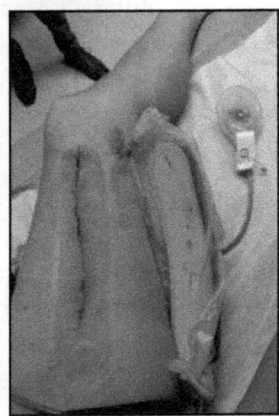

It was very cool to see, yet did not really hurt due to all the numbness. I guess many people faint when they remove them. Once the tube was out, we took some really cool pictures, and he gave me instructions on how to care for it. He said it would continue to drain for few more days. Ironically, as I was walking out, fluid began to run down my leg already. I needed gauze and a wrap to soak it up. Dr. Long said that should last a few more days and then be done. It was weird walking out with just a thigh wrap on and not a full leg wrap. I felt free!!!! I actually walked in with a walker and walked out on my own two feet. It felt good, although my gate was off. Baby steps for now and do not lift that leg up. OUCH, YIKES, OH NO, SHIT, F_ _ _ and WOW because it pinched, burned, stung all at once like crazy. Like your finger in a light socket. I have to be very conscious of my walking now. Part of rehab and my healing process, I guess. You are never going to believe what we did next? Well, remember I mentioned one of the things I wanted to do with Mom during my recovery? It was to ride in the electric carts at Giant Eagle while we shopped, listen to them backing up and play hide and seek. Yep, you guessed it. We did, and it was so much fun! At one point I lost her, looked up found her orange flag, called out to her, and she popped her head up, and I snapped her picture. We had someone else take our picture with our carts full before checkout. As I was sitting in an isle waiting for Mom, a man walked past me, saw my white bandage and said, "Looks like you hurt yourself." I, in turn, replied, "Yep, cancer surgery." The look on his face was priceless. Not something he was expecting to hear. At least, he made a comment. He also said he would pray for me. I thanked him. I love to see reactions from different people, makes life interesting. I even ran into the kid's old daycare teacher Mrs. Zander, and she was amazed at me. I think this will be one of the biggest memories in my life; plus, when we got home we ate sushi, hung out, watched movies and baked banana muffins together. Again, a day I will never forget. Thank you, Mom.

CART CHASING WITH MOM

As the day turned into evening and evening into night, I found myself completing small tasks and feeling so accomplished. I had to take many breaks in between, but at least it is a start of getting back to my life. I have to remember to go slow. I need to heal, but I know Mom will keep me in check. She knows what I'm like. Tomorrow we also need to check out the new rash on the back of my thigh as well as the big bruise on the back of my calf. That definitely explains why my calf has been hurting so much. Definitely an Oxy kind of night.

AUG. 22

I woke up today with what I am going to call zingers. Jolts of pain that remind me of sticking my finger in a light socket, not fun. I have been doing a few more things around the house like the dishes, making brownies, cleaning up a bit and laundry. After waking, I took the bandage off the drainage hole. To my surprise, it seemed to have stopped. I figured I would let the fresh air at it for a while until I was cleaning up the newspaper, and it started literally gushing out onto the floor and down my leg like in the movies. I thought, "OMG! Now that is really cool." I guess it is not finished, and I re-wrapped it with more gauze.

I had PT with Nikki from 12:00 PM-1:00 PM today. She wasn't at all shocked that I was getting packages off the porch when she arrived, but of course Mom was still down stairs. Shhhh! Nikki reviewed with me a few more exercises, gave me well wishes and she was on her way. Short lived PT, but I think we all thought it would be. I actually almost felt bad she came out the two times. Who would have thought I would be getting around so well so soon? Now about the shock treatment I have been receiving today, it has to stop and fast!

AUG. 25

So why am I deserving the electric shock treatments I have been receiving?????

WTF! OMFG! WOW! YOWZA! I have been working on my therapy and stretches, and it is going ok. The nights are a bit more difficult to sleep due to the area hitting the pillow and pushing against it; it's painful. Thank goodness for Oxy! I've been walking more on my own which is a great thing. It's so weird because a good portion of the area around my knee is totally numb, but at times it feels like ants crawling on it, and I even have to look down to make sure nothing is actually on my leg. It's so bizarre. Although a bit of pinching, I was actually able to climb two stairs normally today. Hey, it's a start.

AUG. 26

So today I am feeling pretty good. Got up and did a little upper body workout and my stretches. Going to be at it in no time!!!! I am still getting some zingers and pinches, but walking better. Woohoo. Gotta keep myself in check, so I don't go backwards!

AUG. 27

So much for pretty good, I think I overdid it yesterday. My knee is swollen and my leg is aching today. One bad day out of the last several months isn't too bad, I have to say! Rest, rest, rest. I must keep myself in check. The numbing has slightly decreased, yet I am feeling some terrible bruising which has seemed to develop. No ants are crawling on my skin today, just a few phantom touches. They feel so weird. I have to keep reminding myself it has not even been two weeks post surgery. I am doing great so far. Mom keeps asking where my cane is. Lol.

RECOVERY POST SURGERY

1 week   1.5 weeks   2 weeks

3 weeks   4 weeks   5 weeks

6 weeks   7 weeks   8 weeks

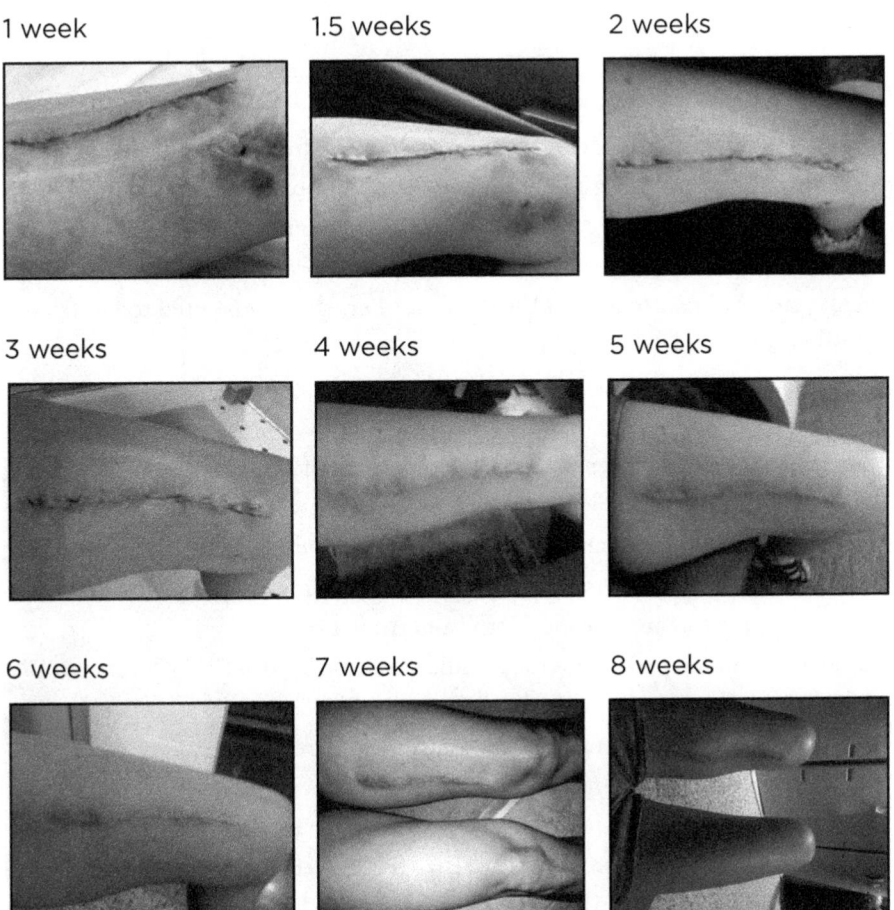

AUG. 28

I am merely MUNDANE now as Dr. Getty put it today! Never a unicorn, always a zebra and now MUNDANE. Lol. It was the best name anyone has ever called me!!!! Thank you, Dr. Getty.

Angie's autopsy showed all margins as clear. This is the best news we could have hoped for.

I go back in four months after additional blood work, MRI and CT scan. A lifelong relationship with my new favorite oncologist, Dr. Getty! He is a great doctor.

AUG. 29

People say the darndest things sometimes, but the funny thing is that I love it! As Mom, Sheryl and I were hobbling out of Red Lobster with our canes today, I began to open the door. As I opened it a young woman looked right at my leg and said to me, "Oh my, I see your scar. I hope and pray you are ok." I said, "Yes, thank you." As I continued out the door past her, she commented to her friend, "I will never complain again." Lol.

AUG. 30

Kathy and Anne came over with tons of blue and gold art supplies and helped me make the best piece of artwork ever. We bedazzled my cane!!! Yes, I said, bedazzled my cane. It has so much meaning, and I plan on keeping it forever. Mom gave me the cane, Kathy and Anne brought the supplies and helped create the middle, the blue beads are from our work girls trip to New Orleans, *The Cat in the Hat* ornament was from Beth, the sunflowers are for Tommi, finally the blue and gold is for our school colors and all the support the staff and my work friends have given me. I will treasure it forever. I have received so many compliments on it. Maybe I should start a side business???? Hmmmm.

SEPT. 3

It's Mom's time to fly the coop. She took such good care of me, and I know she can't wait to get back to her life, especially when I came downstairs yesterday and her bags were in the kitchen ready to go. Lol. We had some great laughs, some quality time and did some damage shopping for new clothes. I will never forget everything she has done for me. Thank you, Mom. I love you.

SEPT. 6

I met with Dr. Katcher today. Not sure what the real reason was, but I think he was just curious as to what this infamous scar would actually look like that replaced my baby's head. Or could it have been to checkout Dr. Getty and Dr. Long's work? Either reason, he very much approved and said they did a great job!

SEPT. 12

Today, I put in for my remaining days off work for my recovery. I am nervous, yet anxious, to get back to see everyone. I wonder how I will fare? Will I make it through the days? How will I hobble around my classroom, let alone keeping the cafeteria in line? Go slow and one step at a time. Jamie, my new principal, has already told me to go at my own pace and that is what I am planning to do. I can only do what I can do!!! The kids are going to love my cane!!!

SEPT. 18

Today was my one month follow up with Dr. Long. He was very pleased about how my scar looked and how I was healing. I asked him why so much of the surrounding area was so sore. He did convey to me that because he did not need to do the skin grafting he had to take the surrounding muscle and tissue under the skin beside the tumor removal area and cut and pull the area closer to the incision, so that he could close the area in a more straight line which made a lot of sense. No wonder it is so sore. He asked if I have started massaging the tissue. I replied yes, as well as using the silicone gelstrips. All this hype about these strips better be true because when you remove them they feel like they are ripping a layer of flesh off. Had I known what it was like before I bought them I would have said no way. That is the worst part about taking care of it right now. 60 days of the treatment plan. Oh boy, I do have to admit I still kind of like the scar and war wounds. I like when it strikes up conversations, or I can see the look on peoples faces when they look at it for the first time. Some are grossed out, some think its cool, and some are amazed at how long it is. I just say it's all good, better than the alternative.

SEPT. 20

I stopped at school to say hello, meet my 5th graders and get my picture taken for the yearbook. I had to make sure I did that considering I am the yearbook advisor, and I set up my staff "thank you". It was a very productive morning.

SEPT. 24

Today is my first official day back, and it's a waiver day. It is a few days shy of my six week post recovery date. I am starting out slowly with only a few half days to wean myself back into work for the rest of the week. It was so good to see everyone plus hear some pretty humorous presenters. One speaker, Kim Campbell, approached me to compliment my cane. As she did, she also noticed my scar, not that you can miss it, and she asked me what had happened. I replied cancer surgery. I told her all was great, and I had clear margins. Kim then asked if I accept hugs, and I said absolutely. She graciously leaned down, put her arms around me, and wished me good luck. It was endearing and unexpected. That is what life is all about. The impact people have on each other.

SEPT. 25

Oh boy, the start of my school year began today. I decided today I would share with the fifth and sixth graders the story of my journey. After all, I only had a few of the sixth graders last year prior to Angie actually having a name, and the fifth graders were new. I think they were fascinated with the story. It will actually take me two days to tell it, but that's ok. I think they are learning a tremendous life lesson of perseverance, triumph and being thankful for life. They even want to see pictures, which I was excited to show them. I left the not so pretty ones out, of course.

As I went through the morning, I could feel my leg getting a bit more sore and even swelling. I sat during the first two periods, but by the time I got home it was throbbing and even bigger than when I woke up. I think I finally have a new name for my leg: "Chubbs". It seems well suited for the situation. It feels like there is a tight band around the inside muscles squeezing and constantly twisting and pulling in every direction, in addition to the very irritating sensitive areas on my scar. OMG! Make it stop already! It's supposed to be getting better and less painful, yet it is worse than the day after eviction day. After lying down for a bit and propping my leg up to help the swelling, I decided to get a few bills paid. As I was sitting at the table rubbing my leg, I felt what I thought was dried skin or pieces of the gel strip. I thought, "OMG, does this hurt! Why is it so sensitive and painful? Why does it feel sharp?" I looked closely at the incision and was shocked to discover what I was actually feeling was a piece of one of the sutures that was poking through the incision. "No wonder," I thought. I pulled that shard out, and there was instant relief in that area. I'm waiting for a few more to make their way to the surface, so I can pull their little asses out too. It is so weird. And just when I thought it couldn't get any more annoying. I'm just shaking my head wondering, "Have I gone back to work too soon; should I take more time; if I use crutches would it help, etc etc?" Today I want to scream in frustration. I keep telling myself slow and steady, slow and steady. Pooooo already!

OCT. 23

OMG! I thought my craziness was coming to an end, but I have to share this today. I had quite an interesting morning. As I walk into the building this morning, a ceiling tile literally falls from the ceiling nearly missing my forehead by an inch. Is someone trying to tell me something? Are black clouds following me? Thank God, my angels are still looking out for me. Sorry, I know it's a bit off topic, but I could not resist. You know how I love to tell stories! Lol.

OCT. 27 AND 28

This weekend I have done nothing but lay around and watch scary movies in my pjs. My energy is pretty low, and Toby is more snuggly than normal. He has been constantly by my side, even laying where Angie use to be. I pray he doesn't know something I don't. Two months and counting until my next MRI and CT scan. Do I continue to breathe easy or hold my breath?

Makes me wonder...

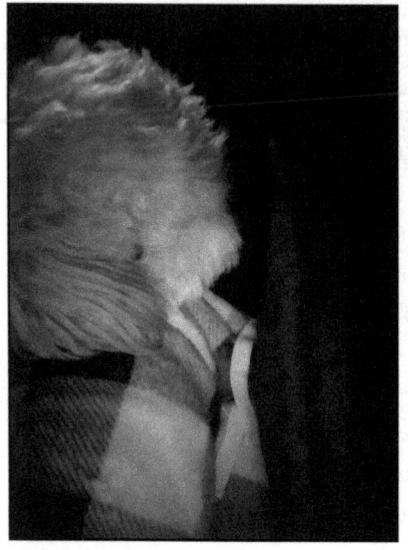

NOV. 2

Wait for it...hold on...

Yep...here we go...not six months later, round two!

Am I, Hilary Swank, Million Dollar Baby II?!

I thought this book would be over by now! I know you were thinking the same thing. LMAO.

But seriously, I welcome the opportunity to get off this ride already! Just when I think the car is coming to a complete stop, I get a little jerk and it keeps moving. Today I guess is an "I'm holding breath" kind of day. I woke up with two small lumps in the left side of my neck. Now, I know this week has been a bit of an "under the weather week," and I have a slight earache, but I am a bit concerned that I have a few new friends. Of course, I was encouraged, adamantly by my coworkers to get checked out, and I did. I called Dr. Rutkowski's office right away, and he got me in within the hour! Now, remember Dr. Rutkowski has not seen me since he referred me to Dr. Getty in April. I think he was still in disbelief that he did not recognize that Angie was something serious. When we discussed what my diagnosis was and what my treatment plan had been, the look on his face was almost as if he had failed me as a doctor. I told him he couldn't have known. Four other doctors didn't know. I do not blame him at all. I felt badly for him actually. I asked if he wanted to see my scar, and he said yes. He was surprised at how big it was. He then commented on how much swelling I had, continued to examine me, and prescribed a cortisone and an antibiotic to clear my body out and help with any infection I may have. I am to follow up in a week for possible blood work and other testing if necessary. I did tell him my next MRI and CT scan is scheduled for January 3, 2019. I better get used to this feeling of holding my breath more than breathing easy, at least for the next few years. It is better to be safe than sorry as they say, and I am nowhere near ready for a sequel!!!!!! Oy Vey!!! Grrrrrr!!!

NOV. 7

So how do I explain this one? Hmmmmm. LMAO! Yep, still shaking my head. My two little friends are still around. It's almost a week since I checked in with Dr. Rutkowski and was prescribed meds for infection and swelling. Well, as of today, no change in lumps or swelling. I called his office and am going in for bloodwork and x-rays today. I am hoping he pushes for a PET scan, but, of course, insurance needs to approve it, and we have to go through all of the other hoops first. Any guesses on this time frame? Ugh. Now remember what all my bloodwork showed before and the x-ray? Yeah, I am predicting the same. NOTHING, but at least it's a start to peace of mind and that is worth everything! Fun times!!!!! Let's see what the next few days brings. This is going to be the never ending journey, literally. Reality is starting to set in on that notion, and I am a bit nervous, I do have to say. I just keep chugging along, hoping for the best, and will deal with what comes my way!

It is now 3:30 PM, and I sit waiting in a room to see Dr. Rutkowski. All I can think is "Man, I could use a cheeseburger!!" This fasting is for the birds. Lol.

Dr. Rutkowski entered with a deadening stare looking straight in my eyes as he walked across the room. He starts writing everything he possibly could on his pad about what he could put down as diagnosis to make sure insurance cannot refuse any more tests, but suddenly stops and continues to stare at me again. It seemed endless. As he was staring at me, I began to cry in hopelessness. He then commented, "You are going to make me cry." In the midst of writing, he gets up, feels the two lumps and asks if I could remove my pants so he can feel my groin. Lol, I wasn't expecting that but I said sure because once you have two kids nothing is off limits. I lowered my pants, and he did a thorough exam to see if other lymph nodes were enlarged. He said they were not. A good sign, I would think. A few moments later, he was all done and continued to write, I think any adjective he could think of. He was determined to get me an ultrasound right then and there. He had his nurse call down to the diagnostics lab to see if they could take me, he wrote the script and I was on my way down. It took about 30 minutes after they contacted insurance, and it was approved!! As I was lying on the ultrasound table, head tipped way back for full exposure, with the wand on my neck, I glanced and saw the two lumps beside each other on the monitor. They were twins, inseparable. They actually looked like two boobs staring back at us. The technician took a bunch of different measurements and said it should not be long after the radiologist reads it that Dr. Rutkowski would have the results. After the ultrasound, I returned for my bloodwork. While I was getting my blood drawn, Dr. Rutkowski asked how my sugar was? I looked at him and said, "I have no idea, I eat it". How do I answer that? I asked the nurse and she asked, "Are you diabetic?" I said, "Not that I'm aware of." Does he know something I don't? As I left the office, sitting in my car, I couldn't help thinking am I going to have to go round two with these little F_ _ _ ers already? I'm not sure I am ready for that yet. After a few deep breaths, I was driving home. A little while later, I found my mind wandering back to my reality as I sat talking to Jay at dinner. My mind raced, like the night Turbo sat on my leg, and I began to break down. I know this is all a test. How well will I do this time around? "Stay strong, Alicia," I said to myself. We don't know the full outcome yet of the ultrasound and you kicked Angie's ass. Any of her little friends don't have a chance either!

I do have to say that there is nothing better for me, when I am feeling down, than to watch a few episodes of *Impractical Jokers*. Along with it, I have some hot cider with fireball and a chaser of Ambien to bring me back to my happy place! So tonight, I sit and again think about today's ride. Where will the ride take me tomorrow? This evening I have also decided that next Friday, Nov. 16, my parents 55th wedding anniversary and my lucky number,  is when I am getting my final tattoo. (Hope, Faith and Internal strength) Might as well not wait because I may need daily reminders at this point, and that is how I am going to set myself up. Stay strong and never give up!

NOV. 8

I woke in anticipation of what today holds for me. Now, I wait! So, maybe Dr. Getty was wrong, and maybe I am a unicorn???? As I noticed my phone ringing, I looked down and recognized the number. OMG, the news is finally coming in. What are they going to tell me? Will all be cleared or will my twins be something I now need  to worry about? Lenore, from the lab, called with the news of not so good results. The ultrasound report showed an enlarged lymph node measuring 25mm x 16mm x 11mm which could be metastatic. We are still waiting on the bloodwork. Lenore will send ASAP. I am having her fax everything to Dr. Getty as well. Oh boy, won't he be surprised to see me so soon? This week only marks 11 weeks since eviction day. Come on already!!!!

Around 5:00 PM Janira from Dr. Getty's office called after listening to my panicked voicemail. She scheduled an appointment for tomorrow at 11:30 AM! She said that after speaking and relaying my voice message to Dr. Getty that he still doesn't think it is serious. Let's pray he is correct. I'm so nervous...

NOV. 9

Today is the first snow of the season and marks exactly six months to the day I found out Angie actually had a name and my life changed forever. My fingers and toes are crossed that I don't have to think of names for the twins too. Tommi is going with me for moral support and an extra pair of ears. Keep me on track, Tommi, and don't let me stray. Staying calm and focused!

When we arrived at Dr. Getty's office, we were taken back pretty quickly and shown into an exam room. Dr. Getty entered a few moments later. I said, "Dr. Getty, you gotta give me something. I need peace of mind!" After having me tell him about how the twins arrived, he did a neck and clavicle exam. He said he did not feel anything that would lead him to believe that the enlarged lymph nodes, the twins, were related to my leg at all. He, in fact, reassured me that he has never seen a case where isolated sarcoma spreads to lymph nodes. "Thank God!" I thought with a sigh of relief. I gave him a copy of my bloodwork results which showed a few numbers off and anemia. He said he really wasn't concerned except the anemic part. Dr. Getty still sensed my urgency of peace of mind, so he decided to give a call to his colleague, head and neck cancer specialist Dr. Rod Rezaee, to see if he would follow up my case. A little while later, I received a call from Dr. Getty himself telling me the great news! Dr. Rezaee agreed to see me next week, Friday, Nov. 16, to make sure everything checks out 100%. I am praying; I need my sanity back!

NOV. 10 AND 11

Well, it's official! I literally just slept half my weekend away, 24 of the 48 hours. I guess I needed it. Is my body listening to my brain or is my brain listening to my body? I am looking forward to great news this coming week. My follow up is Tuesday with Dr. Long, and Friday with Dr. Rezaee. Lets pray they both clear me. My next tests are scheduled for Jan. 3, 2019.

NOV. 13

OMG! I ended up in a major zinger shit storm last night! Worst storm ever! Thanks for sticking by my side Toby and riding them out with me.

Today is three months post eviction day follow up with Dr. Long. How much longer will he tell me these will last? I'm so over these already! They take my breath away and not in a good way either. When I arrived, I gave the nurse a copy of my bloodwork and ultrasound results. After examining my leg, Dr. Long told me that all looks good! He told me the zingers will last for a while yet, as well as all the other symptoms, for probably six months or better before being totally healed. He mentioned possibly learning biofeedback or even medication to help the zingers if they progress or worsen. Once we finished discussing my leg, Dr. Long inquired and examined my neck. He gave me reassurance that Dr. Rezaee would be able to get down to the bottom of my new friends. Before leaving the exam room he asked, "Where is the cane?" He actually remembered I bedazzled it! How funny is that? I must have been the first. I said I haven't used it for quite a while. I think he was looking forward to seeing it again. I'll bring it back Feb. 12, 2019, on my six month follow up just so he can see it again for shits and giggles!

God, I can't wait! Friday is going to be another day to celebrate! Only three more days to wait until my last journal entry. Hoping, praying and positive thoughts!

NOV. 15

One more day!!!!! I think I may explode waiting for tomorrow.

This morning the roads are pretty slick and icy. As I cautiously drove into work, I thought to myself, if cancer didn't kill me there is no way these icy roads are taking me out! The crazy things I think about now. Lol.

NOV. 16

Today I woke feeling scared, nervous yet optimistic! I need my sanity back. I am going to
keep my mind as busy as possible and prepare
to focus completely when Kathy and I meet
with Dr. Rezaee today. God, I pray there isn't
a round two.

9:32 AM tic toc, tic toc, tic toc...
When Kathy and I arrived at the office, we
were greeted by a nice receptionist. She had
me fill out paperwork then we waited for the nurse to call my name. Once I
entered the hallway, she took my vitals. I swear these past two weeks my blood
pressure has been higher than my whole entire life. I guess a roller coaster can
do that to you. I think Cedar Point even has signs posting about blood pressure and not riding their rides if it's too high. Lol. After quite a lengthy wait,
an intern entered the room and introduced himself. He asked me a series of
questions trying to gather as much information as possible before examining
my neck, throat and mouth. After he was finished with questioning me and the
exam, he left the room and a few moments later returned with Dr. Rezaee. As
Dr. Rezaee walked in the room I recognized him right away. He looked just like
his picture and his video online. I always check out my doctors online before I
see them. I know it's a bit creepy, but I want to know about them before meeting
them and putting their hands on me. Dr. Rezaee began to ask me a few more
questions, then began to examine my neck, throat and mouth as well. He said
he did not feel anything out of the ordinary and thinks the lumps are my lymph
nodes due to the virus I previously had a few weeks ago, but wasn't positive. To
be safe he is ordering a CT scan of the neck and a possible needle biopsy on Dec.
4th. I do feel a bit more at ease. So what are these little intruders that now have
forced themselves upon me? Hopefully, I will find out soon. Tic toc, tic toc, tic
toc. Now I wait. The new story of my life. I'm calling it "The Waiting Game"!

December 4th seems so far off...

NOV. 20

Grandparents Day at school. Damn, I wish I would have brought my cane. Our guests would have been very impressed!

I couldn't help it, I picked the last piece of suture out of my scar today. It kind of hurt, but it was really cool. When I arrived home, my knee was the size of a small cantaloupe, cold to the touch and felt like hundreds of hot needles poking into my thigh. Wow! Maybe I really should have used my cane today. I can hear Mom saying, "Leg above your heart and rest it"! Maybe I should ask for compression socks for Xmas?

9:00 PM lesson of the day...never pick sutures out of a scar!!! Yowza.

NOV. 22

Thanksgiving has come and gone. Yep...still waiting.

NOV. 26

5:00 PM lesson of the day...make sure your students put up every chair in your classroom and NEVER EVER EVER let a chair fall on your leg when it is healing from surgery. I cried, almost. :(My leg is hugely swollen, sore and black and blue. OMFG!!! I'm sure this will set me back a bit. Boo. I am telling myself this pain too shall pass. Suck it up, Alicia. Mind over matter! I guess my cane isn't retired yet.

DEC. 1

As I wake for the last time after 12 hrs of sleep, I hear the humming of the fan yet lie in total comfort of my bed. I feel a floating sensation. I tune into what my body is feeling, and it is in total numbness except for every nerve in my left leg from my thigh down below my knee. Every nerve seems to be dancing around. I now realize how my mind no longer controls my body, but my body controls my mind.

DEC. 4

So today I woke thinking once again I'm in Candyland... I mean cancer land. A big day. Clear me Dr. Rezaee, clear me. 1:00 PM CT scan and 1:45 PM needle biopsy. Isn't life grand?

8:30 PM. As I sit on the edge of my bed, Chubbs dangling downward and my right leg folded inward on top of the bed, I begin to think of how to journal about today. I guess you could say it didn't go exactly how I thought it would or had hoped, but it could have gone a lot worse. Jay and I arrived around 12:30 PM and were greeted fairly quickly to complete registration. Once finished, I was called back where my CT scan was done by Lindy. Before we began, she asked me when my birthday was and I thought, "Here we go again..." She was very nice and walked me through all the steps even though it wasn't my first rodeo. She explained to me the CT process and how it would feel when she injected the dye into my IV. She was sure shooting right. She warned me that it would feel very cold going in and then very warm and tingly in my neck area as well as having the urge to urinate. OMG, she was right! It was so weird. No sooner did the feeling come over me, then it went away. She took a series of two groupings of pictures. In all, it took about 10 minutes. I thought to myself, short and sweet just like radiation. Once finished, we headed up to room 146 to see Dr. Rezaee and get the results.

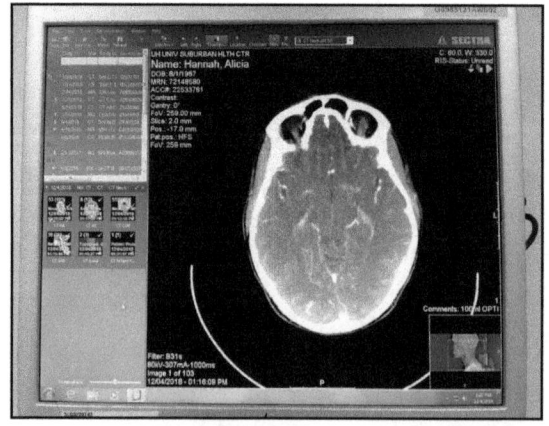
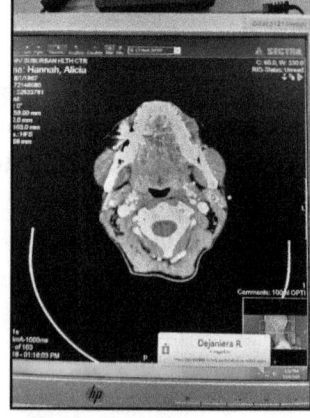

Shortly after checking into Dr. Rezaees' office, we were called back. My vitals were taken, and we were escorted into an exam room. The nurse opened up my file on the computer screen where I got a sneak peak of my CT scan. I, of course, had no clue of what I was looking at, but all I knew is that it was my head and neck and it looked cool. I snapped a picture of the screen for good measure. Lol. A few moments later, an intern, Dr. Vargo entered and spoke to me for a bit. I swear his office reminds me of Grey's Anatomy. Both times I have been there, both times different interns. Shortly after Dr. Vargo left, he returned with Dr. Rezaee. I introduced Jay to Dr. Rezaee, then we got down to business. First asking Dr. Rezaee to take a picture with me, and then to my scan results. Priorities. I had to grab the opportunity when I had the chance! He obliged. Once finished, we were onto my scan. Dr. Rezaee explained the anatomy and positioning of the picture and what the lumps we were observing were. He relayed to me that my lymph nodes were fine; however, it appeared that there was a tumor on my parotid gland. That is the gland directly next to my lymph node. He reminded me in our prior appointment we discussed that a needle biopsy is really the only way to be sure what we were dealing with. Meaning cancer or not. I said, "Let's do it"! A few minutes later he stuck a huge needle in my neck to numb the area, so I thought, and we waited a bit for the area to become numb. After about 10 minutes, Dr. Rezaee proceeded to extract three

samples of the tumor. The first and third I felt nothing; the second one I felt everything. Ouch... but I actually think my wrist tattoo hurt worse. Both are worth the pain! Once all the samples were snug in their bottles, he said he should have the results in about a week, and he would call me. At that time we would discuss further treatments, if any. Now we wait. I bet you know what I am going to do next????? Yep, give it a few days and look online!!!

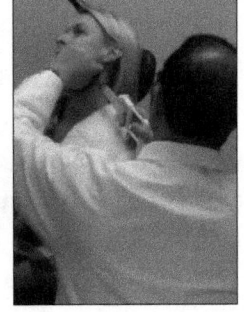

DEC. 5

6:15 AM I woke last night with such a vivid smell of fried eggs in the air. The ironic part is, I don't eat eggs and when I woke for work, my nostrils were filled with tons of yellow yolk like substance. Could it have been from the dye injected into me or the biopsy needles poking the tumor that activated fluid into my sinuses? Who knows. I guess stranger things have happened. Nonetheless, it was so refreshing and satisfying, in a weird way, to see it all come out. Two kleenexes full. I know, gross, but at this stage in my book did you expect anything less?

DEC. 7

I received great news from Dr. Rezaee this evening! He conveyed the biopsy results as non cancerous. However, he is referring to it as a spindle cell tumor. He wants to send me for an additional MRI to be 100% sure and to determine if removal needs to take place. Why does part of me still feel worried? I will feel better once MRI is complete and there is no doubt whatsoever. Either way, I really think this alien needs to be removed. What if it decides to expand and grow and take over me? Sigourney Weaver will not be able to help me then!

DEC. 10

Cindy, Dr. Rezaees' nurse, called this morning. MRI set for Dec. 18!

DEC. 14

I can't believe it has already been a week since Dr.Rezaee called me about my biopsy results.

Part of me still wonders what if his interpretation of the results are incorrect? After all, the report does not specifically say non cancerous. It says and I quote, "While the findings are not entirely specific, a low grade salivary gland neoplasm such as pleomorphic adenoma is favored. Features of metastatic myxoid liposarcoma are not identified. Correlation with imaging studies and clinical findings is recommended". Now, I don't know about you, and I am no doctor, but my gut is telling me that means they are not 100% sure it is not cancerous, and I need more testing, thus the reason for the MRI. Of course, as I look up the terms neoplasm-abnormal cell growth, pleomorphic adenoma, the most common type of salivary gland tumor having a malignant potentially, makes me wonder? Are they wrong again? They were wrong before. Deep breaths and be patient, Alicia. A few more days to wait. GOD, I AM SO SICK OF BEING

PATIENT AND SO SICK OF WAITING! This is all way too crazy to think about all the time. It weighs on my mind way too much. At times, it consumes me. I just want to be normal again, if that is possible. I hope I know before Xmas break what exactly we are dealing with. I say slice and dice, Dr. Rezaee, slice and dice!

DEC. 16

Someone please take the ice pick out of my left ear and the vice off my head. Today has been another sleep day. Listening to my body.

DEC. 18

I know it sounds bizarre, but I'm so excited for my MRI today! The lumps are still present and at times feel slightly bigger to me. I have now found a small pouch that feels like the body of a jellyfish under the left side of my chin, which I'm guessing is most likely a swollen lymph node. At least hoping it is. My fingers are crossed, and I'm praying all turns out well.

So I arrive at the MRI a few minutes before my appointment time, registration was quick and they swiftly took me back. As I was walking down the corridor with the radiologist technician, I was anticipating entering a room off the main hall. To my surprise, she said, "We are going to head out to our mobile unit." I thought, ok, that is weird but I continued to follow her. As I walked out the door, I was surprised to actually see a truck like the old mobile libraries. We climbed the stairs and walked into an area where the monitors were set up. I took off all the metal I was wearing, so it would not interfere with the procedure, then she opened another adjoining door and we entered where the MRI machine was. I thought, "Wow this is pretty cool." They actually drive this around like a food truck. After hopping on the table, she placed a headset on my ears, asked what type of music I wanted and then connected what looked like a neck guard preventing me from moving my head and neck. I thought OMG! After a moment she started moving me into the center of the machine and I started to somewhat panic due to being claustrophobic. I squeezed my eyes shut really tightly and told myself breathe…breathe…and relax. Don't open your eyes. You will freak out and you CAN NOT move! I stayed this way for what seemed like an eternity, but was actually only about 45 minutes total. I thought every muscle and nerve in my neck and back would never be the same, but I made it through. All I kept thinking was the noise of the machine sounded like a jackhammer, and it was so cold that I felt like I was in a meat truck. The things I think about. Lol. Now I wait...

DEC. 20
And wait...

DEC. 21
And wait...Today I tried to keep myself as busy as possible; however, every minute that passed I secretly was hoping my phone would ring with my results. Finally, at 5:30 PM a private number popped up. I knew then it was Dr. Rezaee!!! Finally my MRI results would be revealed to me. Although the tumor is composed mainly of spindle cells, it's size is now larger than what the ultrasound, CT scan and biopsy showed. I can actually feel that is has gotten bigger. It also has an area of blurry and unclear edges and is a bit more worrisome than what was anticipated. Meaning there is a chance of becoming malignant especially given my history. Again, usually only about 20% of these types of tumor end up as cancer, but Dr. Rezaee does not want to take any chances. He wants to jump on this and remove it by the end of January 2019. If we wait too long the tumor could intertwine additionally with my facial nerves and cause paralysis. What a way to begin the new year! As I said before Dr. Rezaee...slice and dice, slice and dice.

So tonight Tommi and I were texting. I was conveying my thoughts to her. This whole journey hasn't or doesn't seem real. It's all been a blur at warp speed. I feel like I am living someone else's life. Am I in someone else's body, just experiencing the physical part? I am not mad nor sad. I am just indifferent because it seems so unreal. I wonder what this experience will entail? How will I feel? What will I learn? Then Tommi said to me, "It's like you are in a nightmare and just want to wake up. It seems like things are going ok and bam you face another challenge." My response, "It is only a challenge if I make it a challenge." Tommi's response, "So true."

Interesting how we all think so differently in life. I know I am definitely different in that regards.

And so the roller coaster continues...

DEC. 24

Merry Xmas and Happy New Year to me. Hell yes!!!! Cindy scheduled me to get this little shit out Jan. 17, 2019. A great way to start out the new year. It can only get better from then. I'm not going to need any more tattoos. My body is going to be a road map of survival tattoos when all is done! Can't wait to see my new scar, seriously. I'm going to ask Dr. Rezaee if he will add a swirl on the end of it. Lol. Embracing what comes my way.

DEC. 25

I had a wonderful day today with my family in SC. It was so nice to hear everyone laugh and see everyone smile, especially Brooke and Johnathon. They were getting along so well. It wasn't until later in the evening, after Brooke wanted me to lay with her and talk that I had realized what had transpired during our first day. What Brooke had shared with me was so heart wrenching that I almost started to become worried that my situation could be more serious than even I think. Brooke shared with me that she had been crying off and on all day worrying about me. That my mother told her and Johnathon that it could be very serious, and I could lose nerve damage, which is true and that main arteries run through that area of my neck. I believe she wanted the kids to know the situation, and they should take it seriously. I believe Brooke referred to it as "the elephant in the room." My tumor was the elephant in the room. I had no clue anyone was really even talking about it. Brooke also shared with me, after speaking to my mom, that she asked my father what they are going to do about me. She began to cry and then he did as well. She said she had never seen my father cry like that before. Brooke also conveyed to me that my mother had shared she has been crying for the last two months about my new discovery. This is the first time I realized how much this is all worrying them. I struggle with how to make them feel better. I can only reassure them that in my soul I feel confident and all will be ok. Do I know that 100%... no, no one can. I just have to have faith in my heart and my doctor. Lastly, Brooke shared with me that she is scared I will pass and I won't be at her wedding nor see my grandchildren. I reassured her that there is no hurry to get married and really no hurry to have kids. Lol. Nonetheless, I am not going anywhere. She keeps asking why do these things keep popping up in my body? How does no one know why? I wish I could tell her. Instead, I showed her a short video of Parotid gland tumor removal so she could better understand what I will be going through. She conveyed to me that she wished she could be here when I have the surgery because she would feel so guilty if I didn't make it and she wasn't here. I told her she belongs at school, and we will just need to spend as much time as possible while she is on break, so she doesn't feel guilty in case something does happen, but it won't. After our talk was over, she thanked me for helping her feel a little better. My heart was breaking for her, but there was nothing I could do but hug her.

Before bed, Mom gave me a survivor stone that used to be my grandmother's and an inspirational book with one day at a time therapy sayings. I will treasure them both forever! Dad hid cans of corn under my pillows, don't ask. Lol. He always seems to make me laugh. Thanks, Dad!

DEC. 28

OMFG. Could I have scared myself any more? As I was lying in bed, mind racing about my upcoming surgery, I began to feel my neck. I thought I was feeling two additional lumps but they were actually the same ones. Hahaha, I freaked myself out. I can tell they are growing, however. It feels like I have something stuck in the left side of my neck, and my lower jaw and ear are aching. First day that my jaw has felt this way. Shhhh don't tell anyone, Alicia. They will only worry more.

I find myself taking in everything that is happening around me more. Scenery, the kids, Mom and Dad, conversations and especially the sounds of voices laughing.

As we drive past all of the cemeteries down here, I can't help wondering...if I really do pass away where will they place me? I don't have a final resting place. Maybe I should secure one for peace of mind? You know me, I'm a planner. In a weird way, that is the biggest thing that troubles me. Where will I be placed? I better get one just in case because you never know.

DEC. 30

As the days creep closer to surgery, I can't help to feel more nervous. With Angie, I really didn't feel her changing. She just looked differently and became bothersome. With this tumor in my neck, I can feel it changing slightly. It's taking up more space, affecting the nerves in my neck and jaw, causing ear aches and high pitched ringing in my left ear, as well as my taste being way off. Is it all connected? I have even had a harder time swallowing. I wasn't sure when the lasagna cheese got stuck halfway in my throat and half in my mouth the other night, whether to pull it out of my mouth or try to choke it down. I managed to choke it down. Figured pulling a big wad of cheese from my throat in a restaurant wasn't appropriate. Lol. I can't help feeling like it's slowing taking over my body. It's a helpless feeling. I just want it out!!!! I have a feeling there is going to be more going on inside than what Dr Rezaee is anticipating from the scan results.

Heading to Jay's Smithmas today. I may ask Diane, Scott, Sue and Craig to say another prayer for me like this past summer at the cottage. They were very happy to. Diane said the church had a prayer for me today. Diane asked the kids to clear the living room for a few minutes so we could have a quiet prayer place. We sat on the couch, held hands and each touched a part of my body. Sue on my tumor/neck to begin with then on my back. Each took turns saying a prayer or helped to guide God's prayer, so he would help heal me. I cried through the whole thing.

JAN. 3, 2019

I welcome the new year and new beginnings. Today I will be receiving my first of many follow up CT scans of my chest and MRI scans of my left thigh. It's hard to believe it's been four months already since eviction day. Let's pray all comes back clear.

As I wait to be called back I find myself becoming more nervous and anxious.

I'm not sure why I wore a bra. It was the first thing to go. No wire in CT machine. Oops... I forgot. Lay down, hands above head, hold my breath three different times and all done. Now I wait for MRI...

A short time later, I was called back for my MRI. I changed first, then I made my way into the MRI room and hopped on the table. As I patiently waited for the technician to prep me, stickers around where tumor use to be, a towel wedged between my legs for stability, a heavy pad on top of my thighs to align the machine, tight belt around my thighs attached to the table, hogged tied feet and headphones set to what was suppose to be country music, but she forgot to turn the volume up, I looked towards the ceiling and thought, "Oh, yes, this sight looks familiar." The ceiling looks like outer space. It is supposed to simulate our galaxy, but just seems like someone randomly poked holes to let light through. It was calming when I had my eyes open anyway. I didn't as much as flinch, let alone swallow my saliva for the first 30 minutes after which she pulled me out of the machine and inserted an IV for the contrast phase. I thought to myself, "OMG how much longer? I am not sure how much more my body can take. My feet are cramping, my leg is screaming and my ass is numb." And let's not forget my cramping arm from the metal underneath stabbing into it and my numb fingers. Oh yeah, fun times! "Fifteen minutes more," she said, "and we will be all done." I thought we will be or I will be? Lol. It wasn't her that stepped down off the table and walked out like a 90 year old woman with ¼ inch indents in her thigh from the stickers now was it? I could tell she felt badly for me, however.

You know what comes next? Yep, more waiting...

I will see Dr. Getty next Friday for my results unless I find them online first. I wonder if Dr. Razaee conveyed to him about my new situation? I am going to call and give him a heads up.

JAN. 7

I am not sure why I am getting so excited to meet Dr. Rezaee tomorrow regarding my pre-op. appointment. I have created a list of symptoms for him I have been dealing with and a list of questions I am hoping to get answers to. I want smooth sailing for this round. I hear he is the man to do it. I'll let you know...

JAN. 8

So just when I didn't think Brooke couldn't get any more scared, Dr. Clancy, a different resident of course, walked into the room. Before she started to ask questions of my history, I asked if she could see my latest chest CT and thigh MRI. To my surprise, she said yes. She proceeded to tell me, "Yes, you still have a nodule on your lung that doesn't seem to have changed." I said "WHAT?!" She said, "You didn't know?" I said, "No, but I do now. Thanks." I looked at Brooke's face, and it was the look of horror. I know she thinks cancer is going to kill me, and at times, I wonder if she is right. Dr. Clancy proceeded to look at my MRI report, but said the language was too advanced, and said I would need to refer to Dr. Getty when I see him Friday. God, I pray she is wrong. I had no clue! How could this not have shown up on last chest CT in July, yet she said it looks unchanged? After making my heart stop in its tracks with this shocking new news, Dr. Clancy gathered background information of my case, left the exam room and returned a few moments later with Dr. Razaee. When Dr.Rezaee entered, he review with me in detail the results of my head and neck MRI. It looks as though the tumor has two parts. I knew it looked like I had twins. He said it probably split and has wrapped itself around the nerve, but he will not know for sure until he gets inside. He also conveyed that it seems to be about an inch big and growing posterior. He spoke to me about what his surgery procedure would be and that he would be doing tummy grafting if needed to fill in the removal area if becomes indented. He was very thorough, and I felt very comfortable with our discussion. All set for alien extraction next Thursday!

JAN. 9

OMG... I think I just threw up in my mouth. I guess I shouldn't have watched that residency video on how to complete a superficial parotidectomy. Gag. What am I in for???? Those little F'rs better never return after this. It's so nasty, and I'm not squeamish! Feel free to watch YouTube, superficial parotidectomy, Mayo Clinic, 24 minutes in length, posted nine months ago to get the full effect! You know you want to. Don't be shy…

JAN. 11

A glorious day! Dr. Getty cleared me for at least the next four months.

He said, "We are right where we want to be"! Next step…alien removal and finish this book. Woohoo.

JAN. 12

Another night of 12 hours of sleep. Getting stuff done around the house in anticipation of my upcoming surgery. I feel like I am nesting. Lol.

As I was filling out pre admission paperwork today, I was asked the question, have you ever been diagnosed with cancer? I thought OMG…for the rest of my life I will now answer yes. I thought…kind of like an addict or a felon. They will always have to answer yes and admit no matter what they are filling out. Okay, not exactly the same, but you get the jist. It was a weird feeling.

JAN. 13

Today, as things were running through my head I was thinking it would be fun to catch Dr. Rezaee off guard and write him a note on my tummy, so if he actually does have to do tummy grafting he would see it and laugh. Hmmmm…do I dare? Hell yes I dare! Now, what to write?

JAN. 14

I went for pre admissions today. I bet you can't guess what they asked me and did AGAIN?

At least four people asked me my name, when my birthday is, why and location I was getting surgery and who the doctor is that is performing it. I started to think maybe they don't even know. Lol. I seriously think they want me as a pin cushion. How much blood does someone need tested in one month? I laugh because I don't even feel the prick of the needle going in any more, five test tubes today. Vampire blood bank? At least they could have bandaids with cartoons on them like when we were kids. Give, give, give and nothing in return. I swear... at least I get to pick the color of my tourniquet sometimes! Oh, and a bonus EKG today too. :) Haven't had one of those in a while. I think they thought, WOW, this lady is in really good shape other than the cancer that was in her leg and the tumor in her neck. LMAO!

Now I wait for the phone call tomorrow as to when to arrive for surgery on Thursday.

JAN. 16

Alien extraction set for tomorrow at high noon. Last solid meal, General Tso's! Feeling pretty well, except for the aftermath of the General Tso's, if you know what I mean. Pray this passes before surgery tomorrow. Lol. If not, maybe surgical staff will blame each other. Bahaha!!!

Wonder what tomorrow will be like? I'm sure I will look like I have a mushroom on my head. I told Josie if anything happens to me, she should finish this book!

Thank you, Johnathon, for stopping to see me tonight. I love you. Brooke, I love you too.

JAN. 17

Alien Extraction day!!!
You're out of here along with your little friends too!

As Mom, Jay and I arrived at the hospital, we walked right to the second floor where I checked in. It went very quickly since I had already had pre admissions two days before. We waited a short time before I heard my name, and I jumped up to go with the nurse. I was shown into bay # 12 where I changed my clothes, gave a sample of urine, got all settled and waited for my next instructions. After formalities were finished, the nurse showed Mom and Jay back and a little while later Kathy showed up to help us celebrate this joyous event before another round of anesthesia, slicing and dicing. Still hard to believe only five months ago was my first round of fun!!!

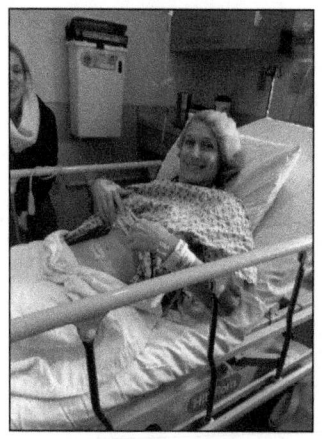

I could not wait to catch Dr. Rezaee off guard during surgery by leaving him a note on my tummy; however, I had to change plans a bit. I did leave him a note, but since mom was adamant about me not writing on my tummy in sharpie, I decided to write the note on a purple sticky for him. After all, purple is the universal cancer color. I then asked the nurses for surgical tape and attached it just below my belly button. I ended up showing him before we actually went into surgery. It wasn't my original plan, but glad I did because I didn't need grafting after all! Of course he shook his head and smiled as we all laughed. Pretty soon the nurse was giving me my happy drug, I said my goodbyes and I was whisked into the OR where I was staring up at a bright metal light as they were strapping my arms down away from my sides. It was just like in the movies. Shortly after surgery was over, I was woken up by my nurse in recovery to make sure I was ok. Now, I am not sure about you, but what I can not figure out is if they want you to rest and recover why do they wake you up just to have you feel like shit and not be able to go back to sleep once you get to your room? Makes no sense to me. Also, before I went to my room Dr. Rezaee stopped by to see me and tell me everything went great! He kept blowing kisses at me and smiling at me. I later found out that those were my therapy exercises he was showing me to do. Lol. He also conveyed that he removed the tumor that had wrapped itself around my nerves in addition to two other lymph nodes. After my short recovery, the nurse rolled me to my room where Mom and Jay met me. We visited, I had some food and then took some selfies to help remember this joyous

occasion. Later, Diane, Sue and Beth stopped by to say hello and check on me. It was a nice visit. Well, you know what came next? Nope, not more waiting. Gotcha! This time, about 9:30 PM I took an Oxy with an Ambien chaser. I thought OMG this is going to be great. A goodnight sleep and home tomorrow to recover, but it wasn't until around 3:30 AM that I finally think I fell asleep. It was a long night.

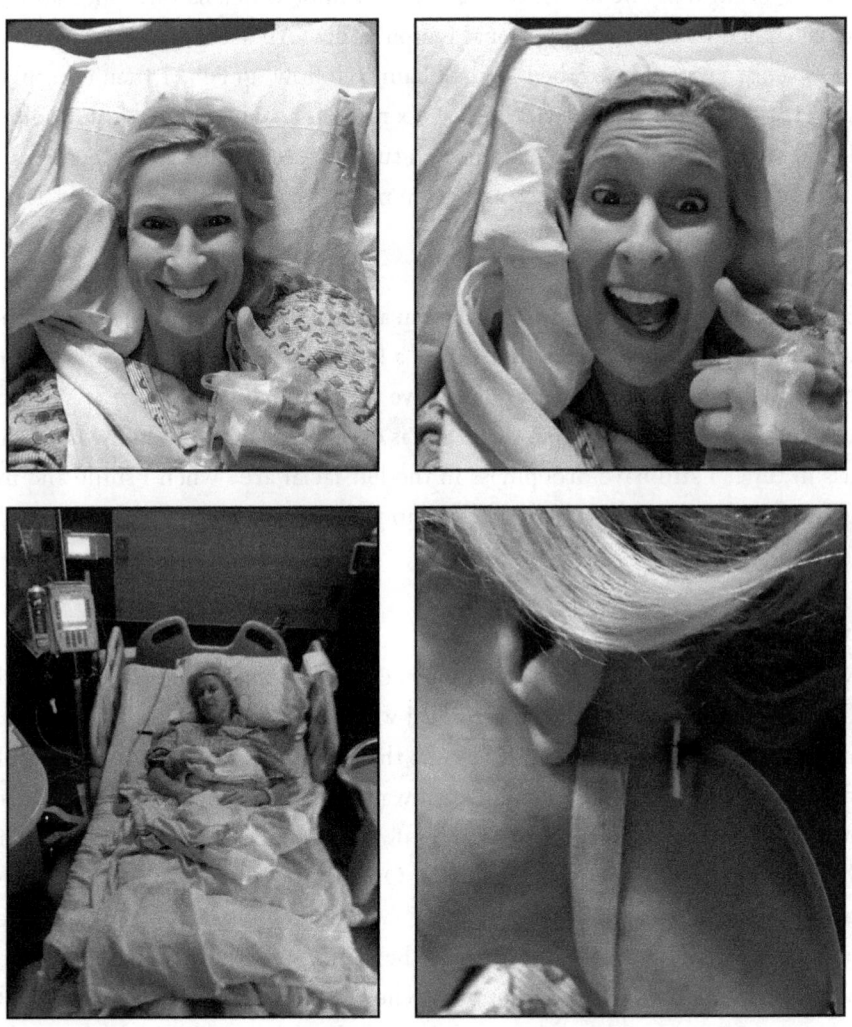

JAN. 18

Day 1 post surgery

6:00 AM I was woken with a big smile and a good morning.

Dr. Rezaee woke me, took out my drain, went over yesterday's procedure, puckered and smiled big for me a few times and went on his way. He said everything went well and he removed all of the tumor which had wrapped around my facial nerves plus two additional lymph nodes. All seems to be benign, but it was sent to pathology to be positive. I am to follow up Feb. 1 then two times at three months apart and two times at six months apart, then we just monitor. He did say that these types of spindle cell tumors have a tendency to come back and could grow into malignancy and given my history it most likely could. They better not come back.

6:00 PM I am feeling like I was attacked in a back alley. Like I was beaten with a bat in my left ear and stabbed in my neck a few times. WOW! My ear is so sore and swollen yet numb and so very sensitive to the touch. It's so weird. My neck feels as if was stabbed and then sliced and is even more painful. I know both will pass in time. I still have droopiness in the left facial area when I smile and my jaw is huge. Rocky Balboa look out!!! I can take whatever you are dishing out!

JAN. 19

Day 2 post surgery

I woke this morning with such pain in my neck that I could hardly move. Shortly afterwards my jaw started to shiver as if I was freezing, yet I wasn't. It was like an uncontrollable nerve spasm. It felt like those wind up teeth you set on a table and they hop around. I wish I could say it was funny this time, but I was far from laughing. I actually wanted to cry and a few moments later it stopped, thank God. I slept most of the day on and off. Once I finally woke, I found my way to eating lunch. I made myself a yummy salad and a piece of cornbread. After dressing my salad with Italian dressing, I began to eat and was only able to open my mouth partially. I felt the front of my chest become wet and thought, "OMG did I just miss my mouth or did the dressing splatter on me"? To my surprise, I reached up and touched the side of my face with a napkin and fluid was running down the side of my face exiting the drain hole. Yeah, I know... gross. Nothing grosses me out any more. The rest of the night Mom and I hung out watching movies. At times the stinging and burning was so bad in my face it felt like lemon juice was being poured into my wounds. The only thing to help the pain subside was ice and praying a Tramadol and an Ambien chaser did the rest, so at least I can sleep. Well, I'll let you know on how well they did together.

JAN. 20
Day 3 post surgery
Apparently they didn't. At 4:45 AM I woke to uncontrollable convulsing of excruciating painful shivering of my lower jaw along with almost unbearable stabbing, burning and pinching pains from my left ear down to the center of my neck. As I reached to feel the area, I gently laid my left hand on top of the whole area and it was hot to the touch, swollen enough to fill my palm and very sensitive. I may need to forget trying to move my neck today and try to sleep more.

11:00 AM Final woke up again with another bout of this morning's torture. Lost the drainage pad somewhere in my bed. It will show up eventually, I'm sure. Lol. The pain is almost unbearable today. Someone, I beg you please take the F_ _ _ing ice pick out of my ear and back the truck tire off of my head. What did I do to deserve such pain???? I can barely get my mouth open today and only soft foods. This is the worst day of this recovery yet. I keep reminding myself, every minute that passes is one minute closer to being healed. Don't give up and stay strong! It will be over soon and all will be a faded memory. However, in the back of my mind I know I will never forget this torturous pain.

JAN. 21
Day 4 post surgery
For all of you who have ever wondered how long a pill takes to dissolve that becomes lodged in your throat, it is approx 15 minutes. Yeah, don't try this at home. I couldn't swallow it down nor could I cough it up. Just had to wait it out. My jaw only opens a limited distance now. Not fun. And never lift your head straight up off a pillow after neck surgery. Do the two handed lift up or the side roll maneuver. Trust me on these. Shoot me! 11:00 AM and I fell back asleep

twice already. I'm hungry but afraid to eat. Only liquid and very soft food for a while. This too shall pass.

I was feeling off this afternoon like a migraine was creeping on, so another nap.

11:00 PM neck still red, hot, swollen, very sensitive to the touch along with some stabbing and pinching. Drain is finally closed and incision area should be set. Finally time to take a shower!!!!

Woohoo!!! The highlight of my past four days.

JAN. 22

Day 5 post surgery

Yay! Snow day. Lucking out not needing to use a sick day today. At this point I am going to try and start banking them again. You never know how many I may need next school year. Bad to think that way, but you never know.

So today I woke at 1:00 PM feeling a bit better. Twelve hours of sleep was needed. The swelling seems to have gone down some yet the redness and sensitivity still seems to be present. I was able to open my jaw wider this morning to get a good brushing, but I still can't floss. I plan to stay with liquids and soft foods for a few more days.

I received a message from Dr. Rezaee today!!! According to pathology report there were three tumors in total that they removed during surgery. 1.) Left jugular lymph node measuring 1.2 cm x .14 cm x .2 cm 2.) Left parotid tumor, left superficial parotidectomy, Pleomorphic Adenoma and one lymph node measuring 3.5 cm x 2.3 cm x 1.8 cm and 3.) Tissue anterior to left parotid tumor measuring 0.5 cm x 0.2cm x 0 .2 cm. All 3 tumors came back benign!!!! Praise the Lord. Now let's get the shit healed and move on!

JAN. 23

Day 6 post recovery

The swelling, redness, pain and sensitivity are all still about the same. I made a call to Cindy, Dr. Rezaee' s nurse to check to see if my symptoms are normal. Also, the past three days, after wearing my glasses, and the earpiece sitting on the top of my ear, I have what feels like on sets of migraines. My ear becomes engulfed with sharp stabbing pains and my vision partially closes off on the edges of my peripheral vision, then the gray static spots come and blind me. Almost like watching static on the old black and white TV. (Twilight Zone) Once I lose my vision, there is literally nothing I can do but lay down and wait it out.

JAN. 24

Lucky #7

My best day of recovery so far! The redness and swelling is going down even though I still have a lot of ear pain and pinching and burning in my neck. I can hardly wear my glasses but have rigged a T.P. cushion for behind the top of my ear for now, which despite my effort, doesn't seem to be working. I pray it doesn't stay like this. The glasses push on the nerve, and it is debilitating. I have to be able to see. Despite these few setbacks, I was able to get out and enjoy lunch and a movie with Mom. Also, remember my drain hole gauze that fell off while I was sleeping? I found it in my bed, and tonight I was able to FLOSS!!!!!!! Woohoo. A great day indeed!

JAN. 25

Do you ever wish you could detach a part or half your body? At times I feel like Miss Frankenstein getting electrocuted. I'm sure it is quite hilarious to watch me react to a zinger in my neck immediately followed by one in my leg or visa versa or better yet, simultaneously. Bahaha. I bet I could be on a comedy show when that happens. I can only imagine the look on peoples faces if it happened while I am out in public.

The dancing ants have started on my ear today. You know the phantom tickles that feel like there is something crawling on you but there really isn't anything there? So weird.

I thank the Lord my pain has been pretty tolerable today! On an upward swing!

JAN. 26

From now on I am wearing headgear when I dust. I hit my ear on the side of the cabinet. OMFG!!!! It WAS doing ok today! Lol

So tonight I had the second best night with Mom. We went with a group of friends to Wild Eagle Saloon. The first time I can ever remember dancing with her. It took me a while to coax her out of the booth, but she eventually complied. I was not taking no for an answer. I grabbed her hand and helped her out of the booth, held her arm and lead her to the dance floor. It was so cool. I hugged and kissed her cheek then I began to tear. Another great memory I will cherish. She has been by my side through everything. She even sent Kathy to the dance floor tonight because I was dancing so much. She wanted me to be careful that my blood pressure did not go too high. After all, it has only been a little over a week since surgery. She is such a mom, and I love her for that.

JAN. 27

I have perfected the right arm pull down maneuver!!! Check this out...The right arm pull down maneuver is when someone comes at you with both arms in full hug status around your neck, and as they go to wrap their right arm around my left neck side, I intercept at their elbow with my left hand and pull downward yet letting their left arm wrap naturally around the right side of my body. They never know what is happening. I get my hug and I save my neck from the horrible pain of strangulation. It truly is a brilliant move if I do say so myself. Try it, you will agree!

JAN. 28

The pain is more tolerable today and since the strip is starting to creep off by itself, I get to carefully trim the loose end. I can't wait to see what my new scar will look like. Patience and no pulling allowed!

JAN. 29

I was hoping the zingers were only segregated to below my waist. Boy, I was wrong. I got my first monumental one in my left jaw today. Wow, sharp ice dagger. However, on a good note, the strip is peeling off even more. Another few inches and I'll get to really see what I am dealing with. I've been trying to do my therapy every day, (puckering and smiling) but that shit is not working on my wide mouth yawning or laughing. People can't help but laugh when I do both. Better to laugh than cry I always say!

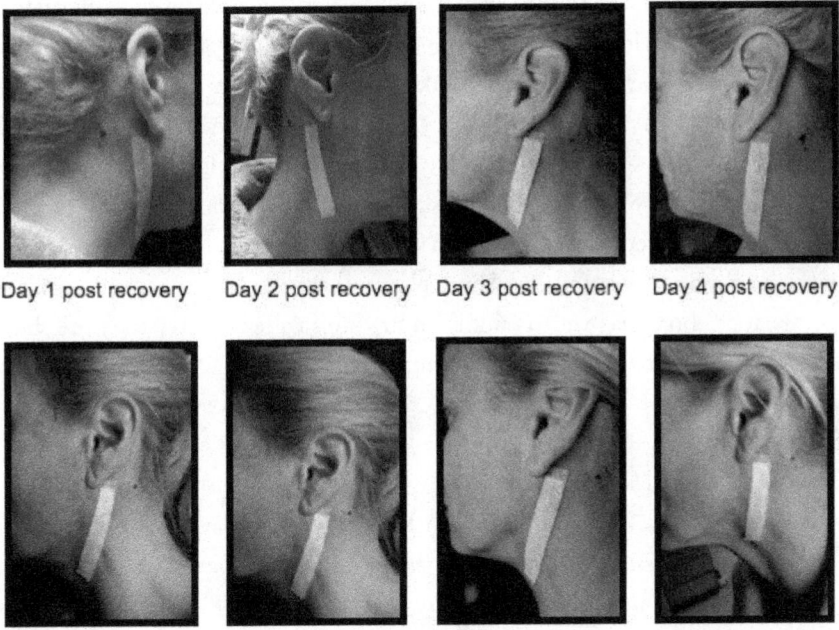

Day 1 post recovery   Day 2 post recovery   Day 3 post recovery   Day 4 post recovery

Day 5 post recovery   Day 6 post recovery   Day 7 post recovery   Day 11 post recovery

JAN. 31

2 weeks post surgery

My neck and drain hole are very itchy today. I'm guessing it's a sign of healing! I'm hoping Dr. Rezaee takes the strip off tomorrow, and we get to see what is really behind the curtain across my neck. After two weeks, I have finally discovered that if I tuck a small pillow against the left side of my forehead I can lean my head slightly to the left without my ear touching anything, and my sleep isn't so bad at times. Not like I used to sleep, but better. Now that's a great feeling. I'm finally figuring how to adjust to my new body.

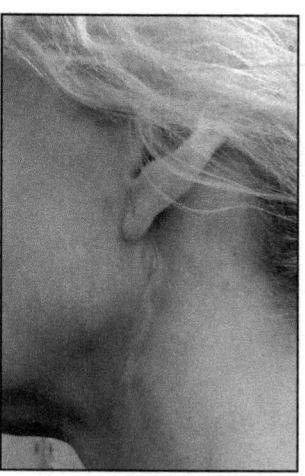

It's funny how at certain times throughout this journey my feelings fluctuate so much. Most of the time I am so strong and have faith that I can fight whatever in life comes my way; yet, at times, like tonight, when my friend Susie asked me the question, "When you think about everything you have been through, especially after this second round, how do you feel going forward?" She asked, "Are you scared or worried?" Just as she said those words I began to cry, and said, "I am very scared." I told her given what has happened to me in the last nine months it isn't a matter of if something else will happen, but when. It is scary to think what my body has yet to endure in my life's roller coaster to come, but it is even more scary to wonder if I can mentally survive it?

FEB. 1

Follow Up Day with Dr. Rezaee

Kathy and I were so excited to meet with Dr. Rezaee today. Finally, the day of closure for me! As Dr. Rezaee entered the exam room, I gave him a pucker and a big smile. I told him I have been doing my exercises. Lol. Dr. Rezaee began by answering questions I had regarding my nerve pain. He assured me that all is normal and with time they should settle down, and he encouraged me to continue my therapy. I have to retrain the nerves. After he answered my questions, he began reviewing the pathology reports with us and gave me copies of them as

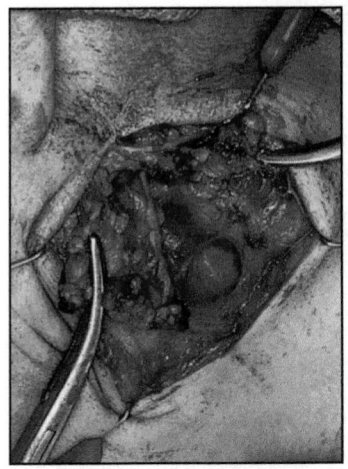

Photo by Dr. Rezaee

well. I asked if he happened to have any pictures of the alien during my surgery, and to my surprise, he sure shootin' did. He whipped out his phone, showed me the pictures while explaining in detail what he did and what everything was, and then forwarded them to my email. He showed me the main parotid gland tumor that was removed and said it was 1.5 in x 1 in x 1 in in size, and he removed it as one piece. It was so cool! After he discussed everything with us, he began to remove the rest of my steri strip, cleaned off the scar with peroxide and removed a suture sticking out. Burned like a mother F_ _ _ er, I do have to say. Wow! We finished our appointment with plans to follow up in three months and discussed steps to fixing my sinus problems next with Dr. D'Anza, and ended with Dr. Rezaee enjoying one of my famous peanut butter cookies I brought him. Life is good!

OH HELL YES!!!!! This crazy ride has FINALLY come to a complete stop after eight months, twenty three days and fourteen hours. I am jumping off and never looking back! Christmas and the new year has already come and gone and Valentine's Day is quickly approaching. Time goes by so fast and all the days now seem to blend together. My leg strength seems to be getting better, although I continue to have my challenges, especially stairs and hills (oh and chairs). Lol. The swelling depends on the day, my activity and the weather. I have now discovered what cankles really feel like and the zingers still have a mind of their own. It's interesting because the one question I get asked the most is what does it feel like? The only description I have is if you took a big elastic band and wrapped it so tightly around your muscle, it feels like it is being choked, add a few daily electric shocks and some twisting, stabbing and pinches on occasion, and that is what it's like. The incision seam is also highly sensitive if it gets touched or hit in any way. Because my left leg is now bigger and a small part of my thigh is missing, I get imprints in my skin along my leg where clothing sits too snuggly. It itches like crazy and feels like pure heaven when I take the tight clothing off and scratch it vigorously. Ahhh!

As far as my neck healing, I pray I never really do get attacked in an alley. The dagger has almost finally been removed and the truck tire is no longer resting directly on the side of my head. Although externally my redness, swelling and scar will fade in time, my internal healing will take much longer to recover completely.

I will forever have follow up doctor appointments and lifelong preventative testing to continue, but I will continue to thank God each day for this roller coaster. Every day, my leg and neck will remind me of how life can turn on a dime, and I could lose everything that is precious to me.

My journey has really made me look at life a lot differently and as myself as a person. I am learning to appreciate the little things in life more, touch everyone I come in contact with in some way and open my eyes to fill my life with happiness. This journey is definitely one that I will never forget. In a weird way, it has been really COOL with so many up and down experiences that I would have never experienced had God not chosen me as one of the many. God only gives you what you can handle, nothing more and nothing less. People ask me many things about my experience and what I have gone through, but the one question that sticks in my mind the most was on Aug. 6, 2018, when Sandy McCullough said to me, as she walked into the middle school office..."How are you? So I heard you had a rough summer?" My response to her as it was to Tommi, "It was only as rough as I made it". Sandy looked at me with surprise in her eyes and said, "That is so true, you make a great point. What a great perspective!!!!" It is true, however.

My final thought is, and please don't ever forget it, that whomever you are, no matter where life takes you, or what challenges life gives you, count your blessings and remember there is always someone worse off than you. What doesn't kill you makes you appreciate life even more, and remember to cherish every day like it's your last because… "You Never Get Those Days Back".

THE END!

My Funny Family

**A few hilarious comments from my older brother, Tony.
Angie jokes.**

I had to write these down!!!! Sooooo funny. Thanks, Tony!

"You have a leg up on life."

"You can get a job at IHOP."

"I will call you I Lean."

"If you go to the Ohio State Fair, I bet you win the three legged race."

"Will you be my barrel for the wheelbarrow race at our family reunion?"

"Hey, Tripod!"

**A few hilarious comments from my dad, John.
Alien jokes**

"Don't be sticking your neck out."

"Keep your head held up high."

From my niece, Briana

"Those deserve leg slaps, Uncle Tony and Papa."

Well…This was the way my book was supposed to end, but you know how my life has been. So, turn the page and find out what happens next.

MY ADVENTURE CONTINUES...

FEB. 12

Today was my follow up meeting with Dr. Long. He was very pleased with how well my scar is healing; however, was a bit disappointed of how much pain and activity the area is still having. He mentioned one form of therapy that is somewhat new for scars, acupuncture!!!!! OMG, are you kidding me? I thought the scar hurts badly now, I can't imagine how painful it would be shoving needles down into it. I think I will use that as a last resort. I follow up again in May... three months.

In order for me to have my sinuses fixed by Dr. D'Anza, I must first see an allergist. So from Dr. Long's office, I made my way to meet Dr. Jhaveri at Allergy Immunology Associates. I know, you think you are confused, try to keep track of all the different doctor's locations, the dates and times of appointments. I feel like I'm losing my mind at times. I sometimes have nightmares of showing up to the wrong location for the different doctors. Lol.

I arrived at Dr. Jhaveri's office promptly at 4:00 PM. After checking in and waiting a short time, I was called back where I was interviewed by one of Dr. Jhaveri's internists, Dr. Sanan and a resident. She asked me a series of questions and I gave her my background. Again, the look on their faces when they heard my story was priceless. Once she was finished, they left the room and in walked two more people. The allergy technician who was administering my allergy testing and her trainee. She explained the procedure and that she was going to use my back to complete the testing. I slipped on a gown, laid on the bed and she started to write four rows of numbers on me. Each number would correlate with a different allergen. Then she started pricking me, 48 total I believe. I thought, "Oh boy this is fun. Not!" "Now, you need to lay here for 15 minutes and we will be back with Dr. Jhaveri to see the results. Try not to move and

DO NOT scratch." I grabbed my phone and watched Netflix for a bit. Once 15 minutes were up, they all came marching back in. Five people to see the raised bumps on my back. I felt kind of like an experiment. A few allergens came back positive; however, to be sure, Dr. Jhaveri had the technician test again on my arm. This time only 12, and I was injected with needles. OMFG, seriously? Well, when all was said and done the same allergens came back positive. I am allergic to tree pollens, mold, dust mites and cats. Pretty typical in my book. I kept thinking to myself....just keep going. Get through this so you can get your sinuses fixed and finally breathe.

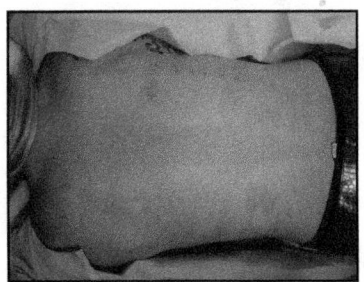 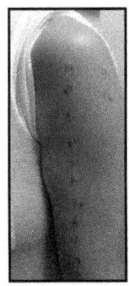 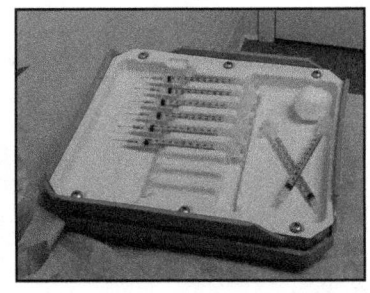

Next came the asthma breathing test. One of my biggest problems is not being able to breathe and becoming short of breath at times. I figure it is because of my sinus problems. I know I have asthma, but I didn't realize how unruly it was being. I was in for quite a surprise. After my allergy testing, the internist and the resident re-entered. She asked me if I have ever had a lung function breathing test done before and I replied no. She had me inhale and exhale into a tube. Next, she connected a tube to the computer and I was to blow out simulated candles on the screen. I inhaled deeply, exhaled as long and as hard as I could to blow out as many candles as I could. I did this three times. I thought I was going to pass out, I was blowing so much. I was shocked when I could only reach the third row from the top. After running the reports, my breathing registered at an oxygen level of only 71%. Dr. Jhaveri came in and said she was shocked. I said "See, this is the problem I am having, I can't breathe!!!" She asked if I have ever had a breathing treatment done before? I said no. She had me use a nebulizer then retested me again. I thought, "She wants to kill me blowing out all these candles." Lol. After retesting me, I registered at an 82% oxygen level. I felt a bit better, but still struggled to breath normally, if there is such a thing for me. After being in the office for three hours, Dr. Jhaveri decided to increase my daily asthma inhaler dose, add a medication to help keep my lungs clear, order two nasal sprays and is sending me for bloodwork to check my immune system. Oy Vey. I follow up in six weeks. I have decided to wait to use the two sprays and to schedule follow up until after I see Dr. D'Anza on March 2. I do not want to mask anything that might be going on inside my sinuses. I want him to get the full natural effect. Now I count the days until I meet Dr. D'Anza! I hope he can help me as well.

FEB. 13

I went for my blood work today to check my immune system. I should get the results in a few weeks.

Today was the first time I was able to put my earrings back in. So weird, I had to play "Helen Keller" to get the left one in, and I still could not feel my earlobe. So strange how many different sensations are going on in such a small area of my body. My new normal as Dr. Getty would say.

FEB. 19

A bit under the weather today. WTH. Tummy, head and throat. Come on already!

Listening to my body. I was a slug today.

FEB. 27

I am chugging right along, feeling pretty well. My neck is feeling pretty good and my scar looks great! My ear and jaw are still numb, yet very sensitive. They are both, however, slowly getting better. Only a few more days, and I will meet Dr. D'Anza! I can't wait.

MARCH 1

I'm so glad I answered the phone this evening, even though I was hesitant because I did not recognize the number. It was Dr. Jhaveri's office calling with my bloodwork results! I thought she was going to say my iron was low. I had looked online already and read the results, so I thought, but must have been from a previous test. I had already started taking iron supplements about a week ago to increase it. Instead of telling me my iron was low, she told me my hemoglobin was a bit low, which I already knew and that my Pneumococcal Titers were pretty low. I said, "Say what?" I asked, "My what are pretty low?" I had never heard of such a thing and was perplexed to say the least. I thought, "Oh no, not something else." I had her explain in detail what exactly she was talking about. She explained that Titers are antibodies in your body that help fight off different infections, and I apparently don't have enough. "Now that would explain a lot," I thought. She said I am to come to the office and get the pneumococcal vaccine and should be retested in four weeks. Hopefully that is all it takes to get my body back on track! Praying.

MARCH 2

Today I get to meet with Dr. D'Anza! Yep, another doctor. I pray he is going to help me breathe again. As I pull into the parking lot I thought, "This is cool, no one here." The parking lot was scarce and inside the building was even more scarce. As I walked into the building, it was eerily vacant and not a soul in sight. I thought now Saturdays are the days for doctors appointments. As I entered the office and checked in, I no more than sat down and was called back. I entered the exam room,

finished filling out the questionnaire and waited for Dr. D'Anza. He came in shortly after I was situated and introduced himself. He had a very pleasant demeanor. We began discussing my symptoms and shortly after he was shooting numbing meds in my nasal cavities, like a power washer, so that he could literally "scope" out the situation. I think to his surprise, he discovered my septum is deviated at both ends, I have polyps on both sides, I have chronic congestion and chronic pansinusitis (a condition in which the cavities around the nasal passages become inflamed). I thought, "OMG, could my sinuses be more messed up?" Dr. D'Anza conveyed to me what he would do during surgery, and then discussed how plastic surgery would work to finalize the process. He referred me to a plastic surgeon, Dr. Ponsky. I am currently scheduled for a consult with her on March 6, at 12:50 PM. I can't wait to see what she has to say.

Tonight I'm feeling like someone stuck plugs up my nose and water is filling up my head. I can still hear the crackling sounds in my ears along with the feeling of a stabbing sensation. And why does my nose sound like air from a balloon is being pinched out? You know that vibrating sound? It's irritating to say the least. I can't blow out, and I can't sniff inward. Starting prednisone tomorrow, and I hope it helps.

MARCH 6
Dr. Ponsky Day!

As I go to many different doctors at UH I have discovered how many of the offices they actually share. It is so weird to walk into the same office that my cancer neck specialist uses and shares with who will soon be my plastic surgeon for my septorhinoplasty.

When Dr. Ponsky walked in I recognized her right away. I looked her up online as I previously mentioned I do for all my doctors. Not only was she highly referred to me by Dr. D'Anza, she has great ratings. She was very pleasant when she came in. She shook my hand firmly and introduced herself. She started by having me give her background of what I have been experiencing. I told her and pulled out my quite lengthy symptom sheet that I created. I want to make sure both doctors have as much information regarding my situation as possible so they could diagnose and treat to the best of their abilities.

Once we finished discussing my symptoms, she did a few tests on my face and nose. She pushed on different areas of my sinuses under my eyes, looked inside my nasal cavities then stuck a metal rod into my nostril and pulled outward.

That was the first time I felt what clear breathing really feels like. We continued to discuss what her portion of the surgical procedure would be after Dr. D'Anza, and then she took a series of pictures to prepare for my septorhinoplasty. I see her again next week to look at the morphing photos of what my new nose will look like. Excited!

After meeting with Dr. D'Anza on Saturday and Dr. Ponsky today, I was given the go ahead to start my new meds, and once I came home I administered my first dose of nasal and allergy sprays. OMG, they were unbelievably chillingly disgusting. You know the kind of medicine that send chills down your body and you want to gag from the taste? The kind that the horrible taste doesn't go away despite what you use as a chaser. I am not sure I can do this. I have to do this two times a day, two sprays of each medication, seriously? Tonight as I was dreading the gagging, I thought to myself, "Two different spray inhalers, two times each day for my sinuses, one new inhaler for my lungs, and a new medication to help with the chest wheezing. Why not add one for my ass too while they are at it!" Doesn't that sound appropriate? Lol.

On a happy note, Brooke, Kathy and I will be going to look at my morphed nose pics next Tuesday. What is it going to look like after my overhaul? It's has to be better than now, plus I will be able to breathe. God, I can't wait!

MARCH 9

I woke up, inserted my new happy sprays, blew a few moments later and tons of blood. Nasty! Apparently a side effect from the spray in my sinus cavities. Thank God for the person who invented Vaseline.

MARCH 12

Brooke, Kathy and I met with Dr. Ponsky today to go over the septoplasty/rhinoplasty portion of my surgery that will directly follow Dr. D'Anza's endoscopic sinus surgery, "roto rootering" procedure. Dr. Ponsky showed us projected morphed pictures specifically designed for my facial structure for the septum and nasal reconstruction portion. We also discussed the procedure and follow up care. It was a quick and exciting appointment! CT scan tomorrow, wait for insurance approval and then coordination of the doctor's schedules. I am hoping for sooner rather than later.

MARCH 13

OMFG! So not that my ear can stand any more zingers or pain, shortly after I arrive for my CT scan the technician called me back. I remembered to remove my earrings; however, forgot to take out my bobby pins. She reached up to point to them to be removed, slightly hit the top of my left ear, and we both received a huge shock, literally. I had just finished telling her I had surgery in January and how sensitive it still was. WOW! Ok, I will let that one go. After entering the scan room she tells me to hop on the table showing me where to place my head. As I settled in, she begins to put her hands on both sides of my head, she said she was "cupping my ears," nonetheless brushing her "cupped hands" against my ears and pushing her palm into my cheek. I made a comment to please be careful. She said she was. Boy, did I feel like I was being manhandled. I wanted to "cup" my hands around her head. In about 10 minutes, I was all done and couldn't wait to get out of there. I thought to myself "be like Forrest Gump!" RUN…

Now I wait for Dr' D'Anza to get the scan and a phone call for surgery dates… Woohoo!

Tonya, Dr. D'Anza's nurse, called this evening and left a message that Dr. D'Anza will be calling between 4:00 PM and 6:00 PM Monday with CT scan results. Hmmmm, I didn't know I needed the results, but good… I guess. I just thought he needed them so he could make sure he is thorough with his surgical procedure. Let's just pray those polyps are still polyps and not new friends.

MARCH 14

I slept 12 hours today, and I am totally going to be a slug. Feeling a bit off. I feel pressure in my head, my balance is off and I feel like I am falling to my right. I am a "Space Cadet" today. I am forgetful, dizzy and just not myself. I think my sinus pressure is getting to me.

MARCH 15

Happy St. Patty's Day to me! As I woke at 11:00 AM in a cocoon of pillows, I realized I slept another 11 hours. I nearly slept half the weekend away again, 23 hours to be exact. As I lay in total comfort taking in every inch of my body, I realized how intertwined I was in my cocoon. Not only was my left ear barricaded from rubbing against any material, I also had a pillow between my knees as well as under my left leg. With every breath I take, I can hear my breathing from within my ear canals. It sounds like I am submerged under water. I hear crackling sounds inside my head, like bugs crawling and chewing, and I can feel the pressure building up in my ears, all while noticing I can only inhale and exhale partially from my left nostril and my right nostril is totally blocked. Apparently those nasal sprays aren't working. I wonder what it is really going to be like when I can actually breathe? Let's go, let's go, let's go!

MARCH 20

Dr. D'Anza left a message saying that my CT scan reveals chronic sinus disease throughout pretty much my entire sinuses. He is waiting for pre authorization for Dr. Ponsky's surgical portion before they can schedule surgeries. It could take up to 30 days to get approved. At least this time I know what I am dealing with. Nothing life threatening, at least I don't think so. 30 days is nothing!

My head feels so blocked at times. I feel dizzy, light headed and like I am falling to my right. The stabbing needs to go away as well. Some day…

MARCH 21

My head hurts so badly today it is almost unbearable. Every little noise seems to be magnified times 100. My ears are aching, and when I lean down, I get dizzy. I close my eyes and the room feels like it's spinning. I look at my computer screen and there seems to be two at times. I turn to my right and feel like I am going to fall over. I drive and I feel drunk. Normally I would crack a joke about my day, but not today. This is no laughing matter. I am miserable…I can honestly say that if I actually had to live like this, every day, for the rest of my life, I don't think I could.

MARCH 25
3:30 AM

OMG! Please make the stabbing, clicking and crackling noises stop!!! I can't take it. I have tried everything I can think of to make them go away with no luck. I am now resorting to my second ambien of the night. Will this one work? I took my first one only three hours ago and you see how far that one got me. I am keeping my fingers crossed that this will be the week Dr. D'Anza calls with a date for surgery. I am ready!

MARCH 27

At times it feels like someone is putting stitches into my left ear. The pinching and burning of what seems like a needle feels crazily real. At times I grab my ear and put coolness from my fingers on it just to change the feeling. Sometimes it helps, sometimes it doesn't.

The headaches still come and go, and the stabbing in my ears is still present. The left ear more than the right, however. The crackling noises haven't been too bad today, but I'm sure tonight they will make up for it. The nights are relentless.

MARCH 29
5:12 AM

All night I have struggled with what feels like I am being accosted by aliens. One is twisting my thigh in every direction, another crocheting on my left ear and the third holding me under water while letting bugs crawl around in my head. How do I make them stop? I woke literally grabbing my head saying "stop, stop" then I realized I was awake. Such an awful feeling of helplessness. I don't know how to get the noises in my head to stop. Please help!!! On a positive note, I received paperwork from insurance for partial acceptance and partial denial for Dr. Ponsky's procedural portion which was the outcome we had already anticipated. I am going to wait until early next week to call and get me on their books. The aliens are not being nice, and they need to go ASAP! Going down for more sleep. Fingers crossed. Ugh.

MARCH 30

As Jay and I sat waiting to be called to our dinner table at Wild Eagle, I suddenly felt what I thought was a hot needle stabbing through the top of my ear. It took me by surprise, taking my breath away and seemed to last forever. I suddenly turned my head to my right, grabbed my left ear and took a few good deep breaths. I thought I was going to cry it hurt so badly. I waited a few minutes as the pain seemed to subside a bit. If it's not my leg that is still pinching, it is this freakin' ear. I thought by now they both would be feeling better. I'm so frustrated at times..

Here is a thought…if my sinuses end up hurting worse than my leg and my ear put together, then maybe I won't notice their pain as much. Lol. Yeah, right. Just enough already…

APRIL 1

My four week blood draw following my pneumococcal vaccine. Fingers crossed. I will know more in seven to ten days.

APRIL 2

Today I am faxing the insurance claim results to Shelly at Dr. Ponsky's office. When I called to see if she received the insurance claim fax, approved in part and denied in part for the septoplasty, she said she did receive it, and Dr. Ponsky wants to do a peer to peer appeal asking for additional coverage. I am hoping she soon finds out what's up. Shelly said Dr. Ponsky is on top of it! More waiting…

APRIL 4

Today all I keep asking myself is why does Chubbs hurt so badly after almost eight months? It always has a feeling of tightness, twisting and pulling, but especially today after Gracie, a special needs student, came over and sat on my right leg. I blocked my left leg to protect it as I normally do with my left arm so she wouldn't hit it, but just as I moved it for a split second she pushed on my thigh with her left hand and all of her weight trying to sit on both legs. OMFG, I thought I was going to cry!!! :(I feel like the healing has been set back three months. I think I may tell Dr. Long I need to try acupuncture. This is insane.

As each day passes and I continue to be patient with the healing of my left ear and jaw, I also wonder what day will be the day that I no longer have to hear crackling and bug noises in my ears while feeling like I am under water? I know what you are thinking SMART ASS, at least you are not hearing voices in your head. Sometimes I think that would be better. At least I could talk back to them if I did. Lol.

APRIL 5

My head and throat were so bad this morning I thought I was going to choke on the mucus that was running into the back of my throat. I knew there was no way was I going to make it into work. I called off and slept until 2:30 PM. Crazy, another day of 16 hours of sleep. I wonder how my new blood work will come back next week?

Once I finally started to move around, I felt a bit better. I was trying to massage my thigh as well as my neck, as I have been instructed to, but my hands just seemed like they were not getting the job done right. I decided to try an electric massager on my thigh, maybe it's worth a try I thought. I obviously wasn't thinking clearly. I was totally woken up after one touch of the massager on my thigh, and it felt as if 100 hot steel needles were being plunged into it. It only took about one second to decide that wasn't such a smart idea. WOW! I will NEVER do that again. Ugh.

Today I also received a phone call from Shelly at Dr. Ponsky's office saying that Dr. Ponsky completed a peer to peer interview with the insurance doctor on April 2, and they are now waiting for the results. "Fingers crossed," she said. Hopefully, we will know something soon.

APRIL 6

Zingers, zingers go away and do NOT come back any other day!!!

APRIL 8

OMG! I am feeling under the weather again. I have another bad sore throat and am feeling very tired. How is this possible so soon? The last bout was at the beginning of February. I am getting anxious wanting to know blood work results. I do have to say that I have an uneasy feeling in my stomach about the results. Please, God, I hope I am wrong. I call back Dr. Jhaveri's office tomorrow. Fingers crossed.

APRIL 9

Out sick again today. On a positive note, Dr. Shend from allergy center called with great news! My titers are now at 12/14 up from level of 1/14. I said that was great and by the way I am sick again. I have already called and scheduled an appointment with Dr. Rutkowski and am heading in at 2:30 PM today. Of course, I already know it's another sinus infection as he confirmed. More antibiotics and another round of prednisone, which never seems to fully work.

APRIL 10

Letting my body rest and heal. Everything feels like it's going back in time for my healing. Why is this?

My neck and leg have been screaming like hot pokers for the past week or so. I keep telling myself "just gotta keep going." Every day that passes is a day closer to full recovery. At times, I still want to cry in frustration and to think the sinuses are next. Crazy, three surgeries in less than a year. A lifetime of fun. Make it stop!

APRIL 11

Speaking of fun! I entered and won my first, and probably only, tattoo contest at Wild Eagle Saloon tonight. I placed first in show for my wrist tattoo. Gotta love it! A lifetime of... hope, faith and internal strength.

APRIL 12

Still anxiously awaiting appeal results. There is nothing in the mail as of yet. Dr. Ponsky's office called to check to see if I had heard anything. I'm keeping her posted, and she is doing the same. Once all gets in order, I can finally get my sinuses fixed. Maybe I can stop feeling so shitty all the time and finally breathe!!! :)

APRIL 13

So here we go!!!!! I received the letter! It seems as though the appeal was successful! Thank God. I left a message for Dr. Ponsky. Hopefully, I will know a date by the end of this week.

Another allergy appointment with Dr. Jhaveri tomorrow. It is going to be interesting when she finds out I feel no differently than when I went in last time before she put me on all these other meds to supposedly help. I wonder if another breathing test will be in order, and how I will do this time? It all has to be related to my sinuses, I just know it does.

OMG, NASTY... I was cutting ham for soup when I had a very clear vision of the photo of the inside of my thigh during my surgery that Dr. Long had taken. The ham was so dark yet reddish while a deep purple shone through and it had a stringy texture to it. I became a bit nauseous for a few moments. Oh, the memories! There are some memories I will not ever be able to get rid of no matter how hard I try.

APRIL 15

Today I am fully submerged under water. I don't even know if people can hear what I'm saying or understand what I'm saying. The pressure in my ears and head make me want to scream. At least I can't hear all those annoying noises the kids make. LMAO! Lucky me.

On a great note, I spoke to Judy, Dr. D'Anza's and Dr. Ponsky's nurse, and she is working out the details between the doctors for my upcoming surgery!!!! Jackpot, finally.

Today I had my follow up with Dr. Jhaveri. She was disappointed that none of the new meds helped. While examining me, she said she had a hard time seeing the polyps this time due to the septum being so inflamed and that it must have pushed everything further up in my sinuses.

Final decision of today, leave meds as is and no other course of action at this time. She wants me to follow up two to four weeks after surgery. If all goes well maybe I won't have to. Time will tell.

APRIL 16

I received a call from Judy today. May 13 SURGERY DAY!!!!!

Let the videos begin!!! Lol.

APRIL 22

Its official! I have booked more doctor appointments for next month than I ever have, in one month, before in my life.

One pre admissions testing May 7, one endoscopic sinus surgery and septoplasty May 13, five various follow up doctor appointments: May 10, May 17, May 27, May 28, May 31 and one CT scan May 28 to be followed up with Dr. Getty June 11 already. Let's not forget about Dr. Jhaveri's follow up sometime in there as well. Wow. I think my head is spinning.

The storm prior to the calm, I hope...praying summer is slower.

APRIL 25

1:15 AM

After a long day of massive nostril mucus balls, otherwise known as what I like to call "snot rockets", I was woken by Snap, Crackle and Pop who also decided to bring Sore and Scratchy Throat along with them. WTH? This is crazy! Now two weeks before surgery and the meds I can take are very limited. May 7, pre admissions. Staying busy so days pass more quickly. I can't wait to get rid of this crap.

Lately, I have also been experiencing odd fuzziness and dark spots in my vision. Kind of scary. At times I feel like I am going to fall over and pass out, literally. Are they symptoms of migraines coming on or could my sinus pressure be causing it? I almost couldn't see to drive home last night. It also happens in class. They happen at least a few times a week and progressively seems to be more often. I definitely need to talk to Dr. D'Anza about these, if they are still occurring after surgery.

APRIL 28

Today I feel as if someone is pushing outward against my ear canals and rubbing sandpaper inside my throat. You know the feeling when you eat something mint flavored then drink ice cold water. I don't understand this reoccurance of these symptoms so frequently. God, I pray that all is gone once my sinuses are fixed. Unfortunately, there is nothing I can take for the pain right now. Sucking it up!!!!

P.S. Who ever has a voodoo doll of me, please please please remove the needle from its thigh already! It has been almost nine months since Angie's eviction day and some days it feels like it was yesterday.

APRIL 30

Are you F_ _ _ING kidding me? Another full blown sinus infection. Need I say anything else? Two in one month is way over the top. I can't take these much more. God, please make my head and throat stop hurting. I want to scream, and I feel helpless. I'm pretty much a vegetable keeping Toby company. :(Dr. D'Anza called in a script. It should take me almost to the day of surgery. Shoot me...

MAY 1

While I was on Facebook today, I came across what could definitely be my final wish for myself when I pass. Not that I'm planning on going anywhere any time soon, but one of my biggest worries is where will I be placed for my eternity? I know no one likes to think about their death, but in reality we all should. DYING IS MY BIGGEST FEAR, but now I may have a plan that makes me feel a bit more at ease. I often ask myself, do they bury me, and if so, where will my resting place be? Do they cremate me, but then I'm being burned in fire and the thought of that is crazy. However, what if I could be shown in a casket for all my friends and family to say their last farewell wishes to, then be cremated and then turned into beautiful glass artwork as keepsakes????? "OMG," I thought, "that would be so awesome!!!!!" Artful Ashes does just that. I was so excited to possibly now have a plan that I even sent away for a kit. I know this is crazy, but I am seriously considering it.

Counting down the days to, hopefully, my last surgery. I cannot wait to be able to breathe and stop getting ill so often. Bring on a happy, healthy life!

MAY 5

Brooke had told me her last speech was a commemorative speech, and she wanted to write it about me. Never in my wildest dreams did I think I would be reading such an impactful speech. It is so endearing and full of love that she has for me. And it goes like this...Get your kleenex ready!

MY AMAZING MOTHER ALICIA

My mother, Alicia, has always been a very big inspiration and role model for me throughout my lifetime. I have seen my mom struggle throughout the years we have spent together, but I was not prepared when she told me the news that would forever change both of our lives and perspectives forever. The day my mom told me she had cancer, I came home from my dermatologist appointment and realized she was home early from work. I couldn't find her in the house, so I went outside and saw her cutting the grass in our backyard. Although I knew she was due for her tests to come back in the next few days, she was acting as though nothing was wrong and never brought up the topic of what the results were for her bulging tumor that had been growing aggressively in her lower left thigh. I asked her, "How did your results turn out?" My mom looked at me with a worried look on her face. I knew immediately just by the way she looked at me that the results were not good and I said to her, "It's cancer, isn't it?" When she nodded her head, I couldn't hold back the tears in my eyes any longer. In fact, as hard as it is to say, I couldn't even bring myself to look at her. I started to turn away from her and go inside to calm myself down, when she insisted that I give her a hug and told me not to worry while wiping my tears off my face. She said, "I am more worried for you and your brother than I am for myself." Despite my mother's own fears, she was more worried about my fears in that moment and I will remember that forever. I have seen every side there is to my mother throughout my twenty-year life, and fortunately for me, I can confidently say that the world needs more people like her. My mom, Alicia, is generous and loving despite her own troubles, determined through challenges, and is an inspiration to everyone she comes into contact with.

Not a moment passes that my mom, Alicia, let's anything stand in the way of her showing her love and generosity to everyone that she has in her life. Although my mother was battling cancer, she was more worried about how I was feeling than how she was feeling in that moment of despair. When my mom wiped my tears from my face that sad day, I realized how irreplaceable she really is in my life. She insisted on my brother and I living our lives as normal, as if nothing was different, even though it felt like my whole world was falling apart. For example; The day she told me that she had cancer, I had previously made plans to go hangout with some friends that day and play kickball. I told her I did not want to go anymore and that I wanted to stay home and be with her. Although I told her I wanted to stay home, she insisted I go be with my friends to get my mind off of everything that was going on in order to not make her upset in return. My mom continued to cook us dinner every night, be there for me whenever I needed her, and laughed whenever she got the chance to do so with her contagious, beautiful smile that consumes you with warmth that is warmer than the sun could ever be. The picture I have painted of my mom thus far is of a generous and loving woman, whose own suffering seems minimal when compared to that of the people she loves. This is all completely true, but there is something else about my mom that makes me admire her so immensely. Actually, it's what inspires me to be just like her.

Throughout my mother's journey with cancer, she stayed determined to conquer her cancer and continued her life as she would normally. My mom loves to work out and although she had been receiving radiation and was tired often and covered in painful sores, that didn't keep her away from her elliptical in our basement that she loves so dearly. My mom still cut her own grass, cleaned the house by herself, went to work, took care of her children, wrote a book, and made sure that she made it to every doctor's appointment she had. Sometimes things got hard for her, but when the going got tough, my mom got tougher, my mom got stronger, and my mom got even more determined. My mom has always encouraged me to be strong and to push through my obstacles no matter how hard they are. She has always told me to never give up. My mom never gave up and that is why she is still here today. I am proud to say mom has become a huge inspiration to everyone around her and the biggest inspiration to me.

After my mom received her several rounds of radiation therapy, her tumor was removed and her cancer was finally gone and she was able to share her experience with anyone who wanted to know about it. Although my mother felt weak, she was so strong. My favorite memory resulted from a situation that was such a tragedy at one point in time for our family. On July 2, 2018, my mother was officially announced cancer free and got to ring the bell at the Seidman Cancer Center where she received her radiation therapy. My mom has always made it known that she puts me first and wanted to share that meaningful and unforgettable experience with me as well. I watched my mom as she rang the cancer-free bell with such a big smile and so much joy that it was overwhelming and very moving to everyone in the room congratulating her. The moment my mom rang that bell, I looked at her and she looked different. She still had blistering skin on her leg peeking out just slightly past the hem of her dress, and as I hugged her as tightly as I could after the ringing stopped, the applause began. I looked at her skin and for the first time in a long time I genuinely was able to smile because she did it and whatever scars she had on her body from then on out were part of her special journey. My mother wanted to be able to share her experience with everyone she could, so she wrote her own book about her journey and experience with her tumor she called, "Angie," in hopes of inspiring others to remain determined and strong through hard times. There is no doubt in my mind that my mother is the most commendable person I have ever come into contact with, and she inspires me to be the best I can be, not only for others, but for myself.

My mom isn't only smart, beautiful, funny, and kind; she is generous, loving, determined, and inspiring. She has a will that can never be broken and a bond with her daughter that could never possibly be fragmented. What I have learned from my mother's experience with cancer goes something like this: ask not what others can do for you, but ask what you can do for yourself and what you can do for others. My mom is more special than she could ever know, and I love her to the moon and back. I still can't imagine my life without her.

I know, right? I warned you!

MAY 6

So I guess God does not want me to work this year. With everything that has already happened and is going to happen with my third surgery, I also received a letter from Parma Municipal Court for Jury Duty June 4 thru 7. What are the odds? OMG! Just rolling with it.

MAY 7

I received another call from Tonya, Dr. D'Anza's nurse, this morning. I need another sinus CT scan. I guess last one in March was done incorrectly. OMG, I am about to lose my mind!!!! Downtown to Seidman Center after work tomorrow. At least they will have the most updated info for my surgery. Six days and counting.

My pre admissions testing went well today; however, as I arrived at the registration desk I totally had a brain freeze and I was in a fog. I was standing in line and I could not for the life of me remember what test I was there for. I started to remove my earrings for my CT scan, then suddenly realized I was there for my pre admission testing. I am losing my mind. After checking in, nurse Tari came out and escorted me back to the exam room. She was very pleasant and personable and made sure I was healthy to withstand surgery. She performed the routine tests and asked questions, you know what you would normally have before surgery? Well, maybe you don't know, but what seems like routine now to me. She performed tests such as temperature and blood pressure checks, the stomach tapping, heart beat, the neck squeezes, the medicine updates and of course the question...any previous cancers? Tari said everything checked out great, and I am set for 2:00 hrs. with Dr. D'Anza and 4:45 hrs. with Dr. Ponsky. I thought, "OMG, longer than both my last two surgeries combined." I have total faith in both doctors and I know they will take good care of me. More blood work before I left. I didn't see that coming.

MAY 8

I arrived at Seidman Center for my CT scan around 3:30 PM this afternoon. I waited a short time and Joe, the radiologist technician, escorted me back to the procedure room. He noticed I previously had the same CT scan done back in March, but a new one was ordered yesterday. He shared with me that Dr. D'Anza needed a scan with more precise measurements. I said, "Ah, makes sense." As I laid down on the table, he positioned me so I would be lined up with the scan lasers. He began to "cup" the sides of my head when I told him about my ear. The funny part is that instead of cupping my head, he took his forefinger, placed in the center on my forehead and had me move my head to the exact positioning he needed. I have never had someone poke at my forehead before, but it worked great! He was very gentle in his finger guiding. Joe left the room, the machine scanned and a few moments later I was on my way.

MAY 9

ANNIVERSARY!

It is so crazy that one year ago today I found out I had cancer. I remember the devastating moment like it was yesterday. I still cannot believe how fast time has gone and what a ride it has been. The most surprising part is that Monday, I will have my third surgery within nine months. How is this possible? It all still seems unreal until I have my daily pain reminders in my leg and neck. Still praying in time the pain passes. I am hoping my nasal surgery isn't like the other two, but we shall see.

MAY 10

My follow up with Dr. Rezaee today went well. He said everything is at a normal healing pace and that we are to follow up again in six months. Great news, although I feel like I have my doubts at times! Now I just need to get through my septorhinoplasty, have a clear chest CT and MRI, and I will be on my way to a normal life again. I am looking forward to celebrating this summer!

MAY 13

I awoke at 5:15 AM prepared for Kathy to pick me up and head to facility at 5:45 AM sharp!

We arrived at 6:30 AM, and they swooped us right into my holding stall. I no more than changed, went to the restroom and an IV was hooked up and my vitals were taken. There were a lot of people coming and going, but the only one I recognized was Dr. D'Anza. He stopped in to answer any last minute questions and to let me know Dr. Ponsky's status as well. He said he is predicting his portion to be about three hours long, and Dr. Ponsky's portion to be about three hours as well. How the heck does one little nose take longer than my other surgeries put together? Crazy. After the formalities, they rolled me into the operating room where there were actually more people than I thought I had already met, but maybe not. I said "WOW, it's cool seeing everyone in here for me. Thank you." A moment later Dr. D'Anza started reviewing with his team my procedure he would be completing and then Dr. Ponsky's portion. Dr. D'Anza reviewed his portion as Endoscopy Maxillary Sinus Surgery, Nasal Sinus Surgery and Nasal Sinus Biopsy; and then Dr. Ponsky's portion as Therapy Fracture of the Nose, Removal of Turbinate Bones, Repair of Nasal Septum, finishing with the Repairing of my Nasal Vestibules. He was right to the left side of me, then a mask was put on my face and that is all I remember. I reminded him right before we began about my book. "Grab me some pics," I said, "and count the polys, please!" You know I had to ask. When I woke, I was back in my stall and Kathy came in. It was so nice to have her there with me. All I remember was that I was so thirsty and sucked down two cans of ginger ale. The nurses monitored me as they helped me regain my oxygen level back to normal. It seemed like it took forever. I could hear the gurgling inside my lungs as I tried

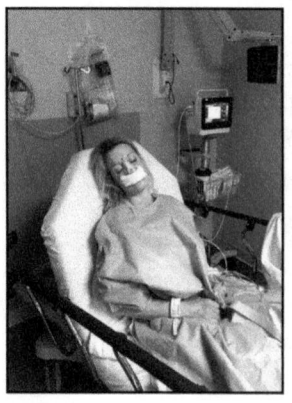 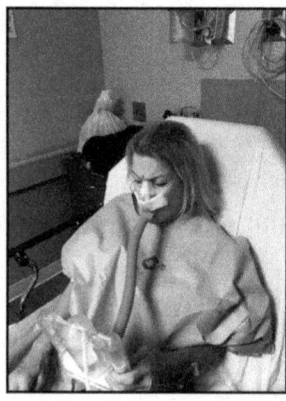 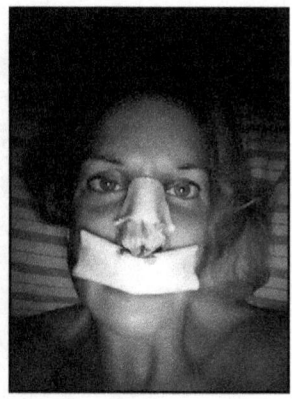

to blow into that stupid apparatus. Finally, Kathy got my rescue inhaler out of the car and once I used it, I could shoot that level way up in that plastic breathing game mechanism. The more I became conscious and the more I was breathing into that tube the more nauseous I became. I told the nurse I didn't feel so hot, and she handed me three huge blue bags. I kept them very close just in case. Around 5:00 PM they discharged me and somehow I ended up with clothes on and in the car driving home. It's all a blur. The next thing I remember is stopping to drop off scripts, then we were headed home. We no more than pulled in my driveway, and I said to Kathy, "Oh no, I'm sorry! I think I am going to be sick." I grabbed one of the blue bags, opened it up, apologized to Kathy and then let the floodgate open. It was like opening a monsoon, not just once, but twice. I quickly twisted the bag and carried into the house being careful not to spill the precious cargo. Once I was inside Kathy passed me off to Brooke, where she escorted me to the couch. I handed Kathy the cargo and that is all I remember. From there I went in and out of consciousness for the rest of the evening.

MAY 14

Today is pretty painful. My head feels like it's in a vice, my face is pretty bruised, swollen and my nostrils are leaking. The worst pain, however, is my lower back from being strapped to a table for six hours. Was there something bunched up under me or was it just the table itself? I pretty much stayed in bed and tried to sleep propped up on my back which is annoying. Talk about not sleeping.

MAY 15

Two days post surgery. I am feeling a bit better today, although I have a terrible headache and stinging in my left ear. My face is still bruised and swollen, and my nose is severely stuffed. The drainage is better, and I am finally able to take the drip gauze off. The crusting is very nasty, and I want to so badly blow but can't. I taste nothing and have no appetite but still eat, but only cold soft foods because my throat is still burning from the tubing. I know each day is going to get better, and I just have to be

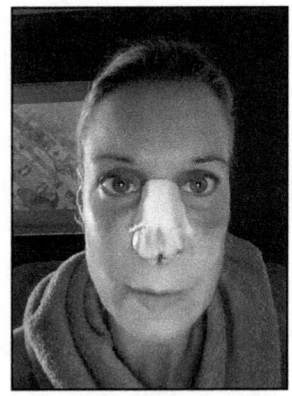

patient; however, tonight at times I get an overwhelming feeling of hot burning anxiety that's in the pit of my stomach. Can I take this feeling of suffocation for another five days? I have a follow up with Dr. D'Anza Friday and Dr. Ponsky next Monday and Wednesday. Praying I can last that long. I have to stay occupied or I won't make it, I fear.

So much for the bleeding stopping...it either drips out or runs down my throat. Not sure which way is more gross???

MAY 16

What a rough night. No sleep. I was so stuffed up I had to breathe through my mouth. As I discovered, I woke up pretty much every 10 or so minutes due to hearing throat sounds or my mouth getting so dry. I have discovered that putting aquaphor inside my mouth doesn't help either. The lengths I will go to. It was worth a shot. Few more days!!!! Ice Ice Baby! Trying to keep swelling, bruising and piercing feeling out of my face and my ear.

MAY 17

Today is my first follow up with Dr. D'Anza; however, I received a phone call from Dr. Ponsky this morning. She wanted me to come in a bit early so she could also check me and remove the stents. OMG, did I jump on that. I couldn't wait! I threw on some 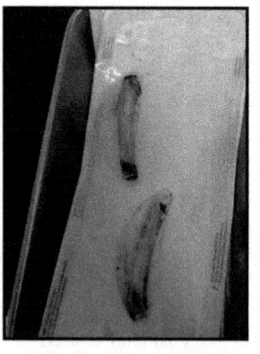 clothes and dashed out the door. When I arrived, Dr. Ponsky began by clipping the stitches from my exterior nasal stents and removed them. Once finished, she was ready to remove internal stents. She prepared me by saying, "I want you to inhale through your mouth then as I count you down, I want you to blow really hard through your nostrils." As she did, I did and then she slid them out with ease. "OMG!" I thought, "They are huge, so cool!" They had to be three inches long. No wonder why I was suffocating. I could instantly breathe!

MAY 18

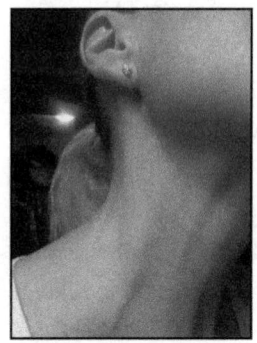

I woke today with a very sore protruding vertical vein in the left side of my neck. I hope it's nothing to worry about. Going to just monitor. It is probably trauma from surgery.

I am sleeping a bit better, but God, please, make this headache go away!!!! It's been two days, and I can't seem to shake it. I'm hoping the cast coming off Monday helps. I am so excited!

It was so funny to see the looks that people gave me when I ventured to the grocery store today. Were they thinking…car accident, nasal surgery, fight???? Yeah, that's it, I've been in a fight, and they should see the other guy. Haha. I just keep whipping asses, but this one better be my last opponent. No more, I'm ready to be done!

MAY 20

I met with Dr.Ponsky today. The first item we addressed was my new protruding friend. She examined my neck and glands and said it's probably just from surgery but we needed to keep an eye on it. Next on the agenda was…

the REMOVAL. OMG, I couldn't wait. She added some adhesive removal, we waited just a few moments, and she was peeling off my cast. After cleaning the bridge and tip a bit more, she handed me a mirror. I couldn't believe how good it looked already despite the swelling and bruising still. OMG, in a few weeks it is going to be awesome, and I can Breathe!!!! And I know what you are thinking…man, do you look like a dork in that picture. I know I do. The price I pay for telling my story. LMAO!

MAY 21

I woke and my vertical friend has doubled in size and is painful. WTH is going on? I pray it is not a clot. I am off to get another blood draw for tests next week, and I will ask the girl there. After all she deals with veins right? Her recommendation...call my doctor. I figured that is what she would say and that she technically can't give me medical advice, so I put a call in to Dr. Ponsky and a few moments later she returned my phone call suggesting ibuprofen and warm compresses. "Thank god," I thought, "Nothing serious." I also have an appointment with Dr. D'Anza tomorrow, and he can double check it as well, relief. I am so over this shit! I can't take much more! I am getting off this ride and soon!

MAY 22

Today, I have officially experienced the mother of all WOW factors!!! Never in my life did I think suctioning out nasal blood clots could be so cool. You know how I love to watch procedures but today, unfortunately, I was not able to due to Dr. D'Anza scoping my nose. I basically leaned back and let him scope. First he shot numbing meds up my nose, stung so badly as it ran down the back of my throat, waited a moment, then stuck the long suction tube down and went at it. You could hear the airflow and each time it came in contact with a clot the suctioning would stop. At one point he was grabbing for the forceps to pull out a few. I said, "I want to see it." As he removed a few, I was trying to peak and all of a sudden I felt something huge sliding down my throat, I leaned forward, opened my mouth and spit the hugest clot I have ever seen in my life into my Kleenex, then a second one followed. I thought Kathy was going to throw up. I looked at her face and she was gagging. It was hilarious and felt soooo good. Once he finished the left side, he moved back to the right for a final suction and I was finished. I felt like a new woman. I know a lot more healing needs to happen and adjustments need to be made, but I feel like I am finally on my way to feeling better. Until my next follow up, June 11, I am to continue saline irrigations with added medications two times a day at least.

MAY 23

OMG, I just woke after 10 hours of sleep. My breathing is so clear, especially in my left nasal passage way. I have a bit more swelling and bruising, but I feel soooo much better! I am still keeping an eye on my vertical neck friend. It seems to have stabilized in size, yet is still very sore.

MAY 28
Memorial Day

It is crazy to think it has already been two weeks since my surgery. Despite some swelling and a shiner on my right cheek, I'm feeling pretty good. As I prepare to head back to work tomorrow, I can't help feeling happy to see everyone; however, I am very nervous and anxious about the next two days and what my CT scan and MRI results will bring to my life. I am anticipating clear results, but part of me is going to be holding my breath until June 11. Take deep breaths I tell myself. There is nothing I can do right now about what is to come. The tests will be what the tests will be. All I can do is pray for the best. I have a 50/50 chance right? Those are pretty good odds in my book.

It's going to be very interesting how I am going to adjust to not wearing my glasses at work considering I can not see anything without them, especially if I have to read. At home I can hold them in front of my eyes, but when I need to use the computer at work I will have to improvise. I know, I look like a dork. Lol.

JUNE 1
Still waiting on MRI results...

JUNE 2
And waiting...

JUNE 3
And waiting...

How is it three weeks after surgery, and I still have a bit of a shiner on my right cheek and my exterior stent holes are still not healed? I keep cleaning out the passages two times a day and am keeping Aquaphor on it. At night, I use special cloth tape across my nostrils as directed by Dr. Ponsky. They are starting to heal a bit more; it just seems like my body is in no hurry to do anything these days. I really hope this swelling goes down, so I can actually see how my nose will look.

Maybe tomorrow will be the day I find out my MRI results. The longer I wait and each day that passes I get more nervous. Is my medical chart red flagged not to post results because that is how I found out I had cancer to begin with or is it just the fact that maybe they are slow? Who knows? My chest CT scan results were posted two days after it was completed, and it looks like no new changes... thank goodness. Talk about nerve racking. I don't want to hold my breath any more.

I scared the shit out of myself today. The pit in the stomach kind of feeling, and I still need to figure out if I should actually be worried or not. As I started my workout on the elliptical I reach to scratch an itch by my left clavicle. I felt the vein in my neck; however, as I touched the lower portion of it I almost screamed. It hurt so badly and there is now a hard numbby area. Are you F_ _ _ing kidding me????? Luckily, I see Dr. Getty and Dr. D'Anza next Tuesday, two separate appointments. This was the same vein that popped out after my sinus surgery that we are keeping an eye on. I wonder if they will both say the same thing? Oh, and I see Dr. Ponsky next Thursday as well. Hopefully between all three they will be consistent in the diagnosis. It should be interesting.

JUNE 4
And waiting.....

I have been calling around to explore the idea of getting my pain treated by acupuncture as Dr. Long suggested and has now ordered. Although my insurance doesn't cover acupuncture, they will cover dry needling. I made an appointment with my chiropractor, Dr. Ron Ludrosky, who is certified in dry needling. I am hoping to try it on my cheek and neck area as well as my left thigh. I hope it helps. I just want the pain to stop!

JUNE 5
And waiting.…..

It is 2:00 AM, and I woke thinking, "How do I tell myself that everything is going to be okay when truthfully I really don't know?" I look at my life as of this moment and think about everything my body and mind has been through in the past year and what I have yet to experience. Even when I finish my final journal, I know I have a lifelong roller coaster to still ride. I am one of the lucky ones despite my challenges. I give thanks every day for being alive. My subtle daily reminder on my wrist helps me stay strong. I find myself looking at it, and even feeling it multiple times a day. I can't help thinking about JoAnn, my boss, Jamie's mother- in-law, and my heart breaks for her. She is battling her own cancer. I wish there was something I could say to her to continue to inspire her and give her hope, but there is nothing. I think how insignificant my ailments are compared to the pain I know she is going through and how terrified and hopeless she must be feeling. Why does God choose good people? I wish I had an answer. All I can do is believe it is for his own reasons and the right ones. I think about her everyday. She is loved so very much by her family. I know their hearts are breaking as we can all see it on Jamie's face. God Bless her and her family. Keep fighting, JoAnn!

Today was my first appointment with dry needling for the scar on my leg, fun times… NOT! Not only did I get needles stuck almost in my scar, part of the treatment apparently is having to twist them. OMFG. I wonder if Dr. Ron actually enjoys sticking and twisting needles into people? I have had dry needling done prior on my back but the thought of the scar pain was pretty overwhelming. I actually was pretty apprehensive, but willing to try anything at this point. Despite all my deep massages, the scar tissue has grown so much that it needs to be broken up. As I hop on the table Dr. Ron starts to feel the scar area. Once he decided where to precisely place the needles, he began shoving them down in, five in total. A few I did not feel and a few felt like hot stabbing pokers jolting through my body. The pain took my breath away. He had me lay for a bit with them placed where he inserted them then he returned and twisted them. Wow! "A few more minutes," he said and then he pulled them out. Not sure which hurt the most, stabbing them in, twisting them or pulling them out? Dr. Ron expressed that he also wanted to try ultrasound, but said, at times with cancer, the ultrasound can stimulate cell growth and can cause it to possibly come back. I am to discuss the needling and ultrasound with Dr. Getty next Tuesday before we really get into deep treatment. I will do anything that helps at this point. All we can do is try. Next dry needling fun is Friday, can't wait!

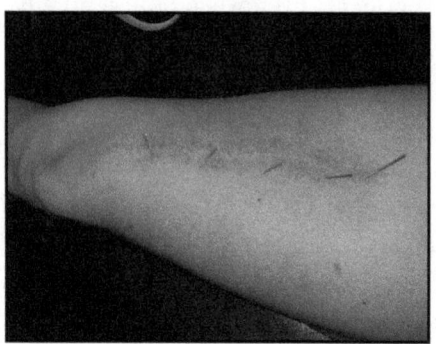 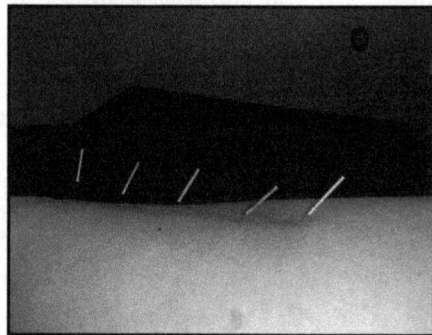

JUNE 6

As I joined the rest of the staff for our end of the year get together at Wild Eagle Saloon, I walked in and sat down right next to Joe Hribar. I was so glad because he is retiring and I know it is going to be a while before I see him again. He is such a great person. As I looked at my phone one last time before the socializing began, I noticed a new email. I opened it and to my anticipation it was THE email I have been waiting for. All I saw was message from Follow My Health. I was so scared, I started to shake. I opened all but the results, and asked Joe if he would read it and tell me because I was too scared. He took my phone and started to read and scroll, read more and scroll more with no expression on his face. I said is that a good thing or bad because you have no expression. It was like time was standing still. He said to me, "I'm not exactly sure what I am reading or how to interpret what I am reading," and handed me back my phone. I put my glasses on, read it again, took screen shots and sent them to mom. From what I could tell it said nothing new had developed. I thought to myself, "You are cleared again!!!!!" Mom sent me a smiley face, and I started to get emotional with joy. I reached over and handed Josie my phone and as she began to read I could see the look on her face with a bit of a smile as she was shaking her head in affirmation. At that moment it confirmed my thoughts, and I began to really cry of relief. Everyone started looking at me asking if I was okay. Joe was even rubbing my back asking if I was okay. I shook my head yes, spoke out a squeal of "My MRI is clean" and everyone cheered!!! What another glorious day to be alive! Now all I can think of is that I can't wait for Dr. Getty to confirm the results on Tuesday, and that I will do it all over again in another four months. The more time that goes by with clean results, the less of a chance that there will be reoccurrence. Remember every four months for two years, every six months for two years then every year for the rest of my life. Two down and a bunch more to go!!!!

JUNE 10

Crazy day of sneezing today. Something keeps tickling inside my nose. After completing my nasal wash, I felt the urge to clear my throat. As I did I felt a hard object inside my throat and as I spit into the sink, I saw what resembled a rope with a knot. It was so weird. I had no clue of what it could be. I thought a piece of food maybe? It was at that moment I picked it up and realized it was a suture from my nose. Yes, very nasty but very cool. No wonder why I kept sneezing, the little bastard was tickling me. I then began to take a flashlight and really look inside my nasal passages, especially my left nostril, and yep there

they were, hanging down like spider webs. I had no clue there were so many. I wonder if they will be removed or just fall out like the one tonight? I of course took a picture of it to show Dr. D'Anza and Dr. Ponsky this week.

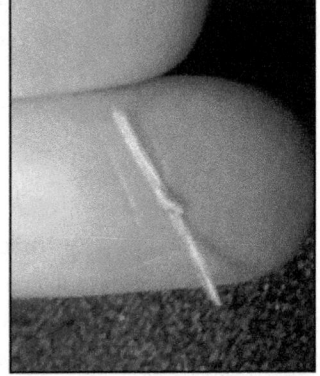

Tonight I am getting more tickling in my nose and I can't do anything about it. It's like someone sticking a feather deep inside my left nostril. OMG, when I inhale a suture flows back and gets stuck. I wish I could make myself sneeze. It's driving me CRAZY!!!!! UUUGGGHHH!!!

OMG and WTF??? As I am typing right now, I feel something very scratchy in my throat. I begin to somewhat choke, and then I pull out what looks like a fishbone but of course it was another suture and not a fishbone. This is so strange, but it does feel better.

JUNE 11

Come on Dr. Getty...I'm ready for you to confirm I'm cleared again!!!! 1:30 PM can't come soon enough. I'm already planning my celebration drink! Today will be another monumental day for me. I will try not to cry.

Dr. Getty confirmed! I am cleared once again, at least for another four months!!! It is such an awesome feeling. I needed to hear it from him before I actually believed it 100% and now I can breathe again. It was really cool seeing my MRI on the computer and my leg looks great. As far as managing my current pain and continued healing process he was open to anything that will help with relief, even ultrasound. He figures if cancer cells are going to come back they will just show up sooner and we can catch it sooner. It sounds like a plan to me.

Bring on the ultrasound, dry needling, massage, EMS and whatever else you have Dr. Ludrosky. Let's get it done!

As far as my recent vein friend, it seems to have taken a back road. For now the knot has disappeared, but I will definitely be keeping an eye out for it to show up again and I'll be ready! My doctors are aware and currently have no concerns.

So apparently those little pieces of what look like fishbones, that I thought were sutures, are parts to a third stent I have between my eyes in my sinus area. I had no clue. I actually was the proud owner of three sets and not two. Lol. It was kind of like finding out I am having triplets and not just twins. I was very surprised indeed. As Dr. D'Anza scoped me, he said everything looks very clear. As he pulled the rest of the stent pieces out, it felt as though he was digging them out of my brain. There was sharp piercing sensation and as he pulled them out he showed me, and I confirmed those little boogers were in fact what I have been pulling out of my throat. Hopefully, they are all gone now. He said let's follow up in two months and cut my irrigation down to once a day. Woohoo!

JUNE 12

So I called and made an appointment with Dr. Ron today. We started with ultrasound, then proceeded with deep tissue massage around the scar area, followed by dry needling with shock therapy. OMFG, call me Miss Frankenstein again because I swear, this time I had smoke coming out of my ears as my body was convulsing in pain. After inserting needles into five different areas around my scar, three on one side and two on the other, he took some wires, hooked up two yellow and two blue to four of the needles. I know, that only makes four. Very good, you were paying attention. The fifth needle basically just hung out and watched as the others tortured me. Grrrr I know, right? He proceeded to turn on and increase the shock pulsations connected to each needle. Some I hardly felt and some were like shards of glass shooting into my leg. "Can you feel them?" he asked, as I am leaned back in my chair biting my lip. Yowza. I said, "Yes, but I can handle it." It's not worse than some of the zingers I get, and if it's going to help

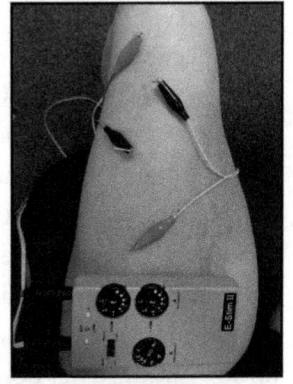

then keep the level. I sat that way for what must have been 10 or 15 minutes. Eventually they started to pull away from the skin a bit. When time was up, Carol, his nurse came and twisted them out. Some slid right out and some she had to wrestle twisting back and forth to remove. I hope all this pain is worth it. You know the saying...no pain no gain.

Did I stop somewhere today, buy a new elastic band and tie it around my leg so tight that it feels like it's choking my thigh and shards of glass are sticking in it?

Because that is exactly what it feels like today. Wow! I hope it's not a set back but an indication of progression. Ibuprofen and ice ice baby!

JUNE 13

Today is my final doctor's appointment for another four weeks, other than Dr. Ron and pain therapy of course. A glorious day it is!

It has been exactly four weeks since my sinus surgery, and it is my four week follow up with Dr. Ponsky. She is very pleased to see my suture holes are finally starting to heal. There is still quite a bit of swelling and is predicting steroid shots but wants to wait until our next follow up. "Let's be more aggressive with the massaging, keep up the irrigations and I will see you in July," she said. She took some photos to see my progression, and I was on my way. I left feeling great and on my way to a full recovery. "It's about time," I thought! Now, I just wish I had three sets of hands to massage my thigh, neck and nose various times throughout the days! Lol.

I know… slow, steady, and being consistent is the power of treatment and healing. I feel like that's all I do any more, rub rub rub rub rub rub rub. Tiresome to say the least! A means to an end, but I know it will be all worth it. I am definitely on the road to full recovery, and it feels great!!! I'm finally getting my life back!

Speaking of my life back, I have a fully packed summer of memories to come. I am attending a Billy Currington concert in Toledo and a trip to Margaritaville in Hollywood, Florida, with Kathy; spending a few days in Memphis, TN, with Josie and Tina; and then an overnight stay in Geneva on The Lake with the girls from work. Life doesn't get better than this!

JULY 2

Today is July 2, 2019, which marks the one year anniversary of my final radiation treatment, my bell ringing ceremony and will be my final journal entry! It is amazing how time passes so quickly. Even though I am feeling great physically and mentally, I know I have a future filled with medical tests and a great deal more healing. I will never forget standing on the rooftop of The Peabody Hotel, while in Memphis, TN, watching the sunset reflecting off the Mississippi River reminiscing about my life and how lucky I am. I realized that after thirteen months, three weeks and two days this roller coaster has finally come to a complete stop, and I have now hopped on the train to recovery. It has been one hell of a ride!!! Although I don't know where life will take me from here, I do know that this journey has enabled me to see life more clearly. I have become a stronger and a more thankful person, and I will take nothing for granted. I feel after my past year's challenges I can persevere anything that comes my way, and I will cherish every life's memory to come. I have always said throughout this whole experience, that it has been my journey, when in fact, I think my journey is just about to start. If there is one thing I have learned throughout this adventure is that life is too short. My life is just about to begin and I say, "Bring on the memories," because I am ready, and I am going to hang on tight!!!

Sunset on the Mississippi River, The Peabody Hotel Rooftop

"Life is a journey, not a destination."

Ralph Waldo Emerson

In closing, if you remember nothing else, please remember this…we all must make our own great memories and have no regrets because…

"You Never Get Those Days Back!"

THE END...

CPSIA information can be obtained
at www.ICGtesting.com
Printed in the USA
BVHW011603271019
562166BV00005B/130/P